Germany Is Our Problem

As for Germany, that tragic nation which has sown the wind and is now reaping the whirlwind—we and our Allies are entirely agreed that we shall not bargain with the Nazi conspirators, or leave them a shred of control—open or secret—of the instruments of government.

We shall not leave them a single element of military power—or of potential military power.

But I should be false to the very foundations of my religious and political convictions, if I should ever relinquish the hope—and even the faith—that in all people, without exception, there lives some instinct for truth, some attraction toward justice, and some passion for peace—buried as they may be in the German case under a brutal regime.

We bring no charge against the German race, as such, for we cannot believe that God has eternally condemned any race of humanity. For we know in our own land how many good men and women of German ancestry have proved loyal, freedom-loving, peace-loving citizens.

There is going to be stern punishment for all those in Germany directly responsible for this agony of mankind.

The German people are not going to be enslaved—because the United Nations do not traffic in human slavery. But it will be necessary for them to earn their way back into the fellowship of peace-loving and law-abiding nations. And, in their climb up that steep road, we shall certainly see to it that they are not encumbered by having to carry guns. They will be relieved of that burden—we hope, forever.

—President Roosevelt

Germany Is Our Problem

by

Henry Morgenthau, Jr.

Harper & Brothers *Publishers*
New York *and* London

GERMANY IS OUR PROBLEM

10-5

FIRST EDITION

I-U

TO MY SONS

HENRY MORGENTHAU, III (CAPTAIN, A.U.S.)

AND

ROBERT MORRIS MORGENTHAU (LIEUT., U.S.N.R.)

WITH THE HOPE THAT NEITHER

THEY NOR THEIR CHILDREN

WILL HAVE TO FIGHT IN

ANOTHER WAR

On the following pages is reproduced a photographic copy of the memorandum summarizing "The Morgenthau Plan" which President Roosevelt took with him to the historic conference at Quebec in September of 1944.

TOP SECRET

Program to Prevent Germany from starting a World War III

1. Demilitarization of Germany.

It should be the aim of the Allied Forces to accomplish the complete demilitarization of Germany in the shortest possible period of time after surrender. This means completely disarming the German Army and people (including the removal or destruction of all war material), the total destruction of the whole German armament industry, and the removal or destruction of other key industries which are basic to military strength.

2. New Boundaries of Germany.

(a) Poland should get that part of East Prussia which doesn't go to the U.S.S.R. and the southern portion of Silesia. (See map in 12 Appendix.)

(b) France should get the Saar and the adjacent territories bounded by the Rhine and the Moselle Rivers.

(c) As indicated in 4 below an International Zone should be created containing the Ruhr and the surrounding industrial areas.

3. Partitioning of New Germany.

The remaining portion of Germany should be divided into two autonomous, independent states, (1) a South German state comprising Bavaria, Wuerttemberg, Baden and some smaller areas and (2) a North German state comprising a large part of the old state of Prussia, Saxony, Thuringia and several smaller states.

There shall be a custom union between the new South German state and Austria, which will be restored to her pre-1938 political borders.

4. The Ruhr Area. (The Ruhr, surrounding industrial areas, as shown on the map, including the Rhineland, the Keil Canal, and all German territory north of the Keil Canal.)

Here lies the heart of German industrial power. This area should not only be stripped of all presently existing industries but so weakened and controlled that it can not in the foreseeable future become an industrial area. The following steps will accomplish this:

(a) Within a short period, if possible not longer than 6 months after the cessation of hostilities, all industrial plants and equipment not destroyed by military action shall be completely dismantled and transported to Allied Nations as restitution. All equipment shall be removed from the mines and the mines closed.

(b) The area should be made an international zone to be governed by an international security organization to be established by the United Nations. In governing the area the international organization should be guided by policies designed to further the above stated objective.

5. Restitution and Reparation.

Reparations, in the form of future payments and deliveries, should not be demanded. Restitution and reparation shall be effected by the transfer of existing German resources and territories, e.g.,

(a) by restitution of property looted by the Germans in territories occupied by them;

(b) by transfer of German territory and German private rights in industrial property situated in such territory to invaded countries and the international organization under the program of partition;

(c) by the removal and distribution among devastated countries of industrial plants and equipment situated within the International Zone and the North and South German states delimited in the section on partition;

(d) by forced German labor outside Germany; and

(e) by confiscation of all German assets of any character whatsoever outside of Germany.

6. Education and Propaganda.

(a) All schools and universities will be closed until an Allied Commission of Education has formulated an effective reorganization program. It is contemplated that it may require a considerable period of time before any institutions of higher education are reopened. Meanwhile the education of German students in foreign universities will not be prohibited. Elementary schools will be reopened as quickly as appropriate teachers and textbooks are available.

(b) All German radio stations and newspapers, magazines, weeklies, etc. shall be discontinued until adequate controls are established and an appropriate program formulated.

7. Political Decentralization.

The military administration in Germany in the initial period should be carried out with a view toward the eventual partitioning of Germany. To facilitate partitioning and to assure its permanence the military authorities should be guided by the following principles:

(a) Dismiss all policy-making officials of the Reich government and deal primarily with local governments.

(b) Encourage the reestablishment of state governments in each of the states (Lander) corresponding to 18 states into which Germany is presently divided and in addition make the Prussian provinces separate states.

(c) Upon the partition of Germany, the various state overnments should be encouraged to organize a federal governent for each of the newly partitioned areas. Such new governents should be in the form of a confederation of states, with mphasis on states' rights and a large degree of local autonomy.

. Responsibility of Military for Local German Economy.

The sole purpose of the military in control of the German conomy shall be to facilitate military operations and military ccupation. The Allied Military Government shall not assume esponsibility for such economic problems as price controls, ationing, unemployment, production, reconstruction, distribuion, consumption, housing, or transportation, or take any measres designed to maintain or strengthen the German economy, exept those which are essential to military operations. The esponsibility for sustaining the German economy and people ests with the German people with such facilities as may be vailable under the circumstances.

. Controls over Development of German Economy.

During a period of at least twenty years after surrender adeuate controls, including controls over foreign trade and tight estrictions on capital imports, shall be maintained by the nited Nations designed to prevent in the newly-established states he establishment or expansion of key industries basic to the erman military potential and to control other key industries.

.0. Agrarian program.

All large estates should be broken up and divided among the easants and the system of primogeniture and entail should be bolished.

.1. Punishment of War Crimes and Treatment of Special Groups. √

A program for the punishment of certain war crimes and for he treatment of Nazi organizations and other special groups is ontained in section 11.

.2. Uniforms and Parades.

(a) No German shall be permitted to wear, after an appropriate period of time following the cessation of hostilities, any ilitary uniform or any uniform of any quasi military organizations.

(b) No military parades shall be permitted anywhere in ermany and all military bands shall be disbanded.

13. Aircraft.

All aircraft (including gliders), whether military or commercial, will be confiscated for later disposition. No German shall be permitted to operate or to help operate any aircraft, including those owned by foreign interests.

14. <u>United States Responsibility</u>.

Although the United States would have full military and civilian representation on whatever international commission or commissions may be established for the execution of the whole German program, the primary responsibility for the policing of Germany and for civil administration in Germany should be assumed by the military forces of Germany's continental neighbors. Specifically, these should include Russian, French, Polish, Czech, Greek, Yugoslav, Norwegian, Dutch and Belgian soldiers.

Under this program United States troops could be withdrawn within a relatively short time.

Table of Contents

This book owes much to discussions I have had on the subject with many authorities, both in and out of Government, and to analyses that have been made by a number of other experts in the field. To all of them I wish to express my gratitude and appreciation. Their help has been invaluable, but the interpretations and opinions expressed here are my responsibility, not theirs.

I have donated this book to the Elinor and Henry Morgenthau Jr. Foundation for Peace Inc., a non-profit membership corporation. The Foundation will use the proceeds of the publication and distribution of the book for the purpose of encouraging individuals and organizations aspiring for a world of freedom, peace and security and for the coordination and direction of the efforts of all peoples in their struggle for the attainment of such a world.

H. M., Jr.

THE REASON FOR THIS BOOK

IN SEPTEMBER, 1944, PRESIDENT FRANKLIN D. Roosevelt asked me to outline for him a program for the treatment of Germany after her defeat. He wished to take such a document to the Quebec Conference, which was to be held in a few days, and he knew that I had devoted a good deal of thought and study to the subject. As Secretary of the Treasury, I had been led into the whole problem by questions of reparations, currency and financial controls. I had seen that these could not be divorced from the broader aspects of what to do with Germany. The President, with whom I had been privileged to work on terms of intimacy and confidence for many years, knew of my interest and my research.

Only a few weeks before the President made his request, I had been in London, and the sight of that bombed city with its courageous people had deepened my convictions, as I think it must have deepened the convictions of anyone who saw London in wartime. It prompted the theme of a broadcast I made on the eve of my departure and in which I said:

> There can be no peace on earth—no security for any man, woman or child—if aggressor nations like Germany and Japan retain any power to strike at their neighbors.
>
> It is not enough for us to say, "We will disarm Germany

and Japan and *hope* that they will learn to behave themselves as decent people." Hoping is not enough.

That was the spirit in which I drew up the plan which Mr. Roosevelt had requested. I know that was the spirit in which he received it. No part of that plan has ever been made public by me until now. This book is an elaboration of the program which I then submitted to the President for his use. It is essentially the same framework, but with additional research and documentation to supplement the much slimmer document which Mr. Roosevelt took to Quebec.

Since that conference, it is worth noting, the basic principles of the program have represented the official position of the United States Government. It is obvious that in the Potsdam Declaration signed by President Truman, Prime Minister Attlee and Marshal Stalin, the three principal Allies were seeking to carry out the objectives of that policy. For purposes of comparison, the Declaration is printed in Appendix C of this volume.

The similarities will be apparent to any reader. So will the differences. Both ought to be considered solely from the standpoint of whether the common objective is furthered or not by any particular feature of the proposed settlement. However, my aim is not to argue with any specific details of the Potsdam Declaration, but to state for the country the philosophy which went into the formulation of American policy embodied in the Declaration.

In writing this book, I have been motivated entirely by the conviction that the purpose of our program for dealing with Germany should be peace. And that should be its only purpose. The peoples of the earth have a right to demand of their peacemakers that another generation of youth shall not have to be maimed and die in the defense of human freedom.

The hopes of mankind rest upon the peace which we are now beginning to build out of the wreckage of lives and cities and nations. It is an awesome but an inspiring task. It is for us, the living, to see to it that our dead shall not have died in vain. Because I am sure that all our hopes and yearnings for peace will fade and die unless we build upon a firm foundation, the foundation of an assured end to German aggression, I have undertaken to explain in this volume just what measures I advocate and why.

Germany Is Our Problem

Chapter I

THE ROAD TO WAR

THE BELLS OF JUBILEE RANG WILDLY through half the world, and all along the battle-front fighting men lifted themselves out of the mud, stood erect and breathed the air of peace. But on his bed in a Pomeranian hospital Corporal Adolf Hitler wept with hysterical rage. For it was November 11, 1918, and Germany's new government of supposed democrats had accepted what the corporal considered shameful armistice terms, read out to them in a coldly precise tone by the French General Maxime Weygand as they sat around the long bare table of a dining car in the Compiègne Forest. Twenty-two years later that same General Weygand's officers sat in the same dining car in the same forest, listening instead of reading as the conditions of another armistice were pronounced, but this time in German voices. The corporal who had wept in Pomerania beamed and strutted for the newsreels in Compiègne.

What had happened to the world's high hopes of peace? What had happened to Corporal Hitler's fears? So many precautions had been taken to prevent the Germans from breaking out again! But something must have been omitted. Yet when a peace treaty followed the armistice of 1918, only a few men like the implacable Lorrainer, Raymond Poincare, President and later Premier of France, doubted that the Teutonic menace had been crushed. The Reich, presided over by a Social Democrat, the former saddler Friedrich Ebert, and living under the liberal republican constitution adopted at Weimar, was on the road to democracy, men said. She was disarmed, and an Allied commission had been set up to see that all her strictly war industries were dismantled. She had lost Alsace and Lorraine, the Saar basin, other bits and pieces in the west annexed to Belgium and Denmark; she had lost parts of Silesia, the Polish Corridor, Danzig, Memel. She was bound to a heavy schedule of reparations. She was under obligation to deliver to the Allies for trial those of her citizens who had plotted and committed the crime of war. The Rhineland was occupied by Allied troops to insure good behavior, and occupation of other areas might follow bad.

But Germany kept intact far more powerful forces for evil than those she lost. She kept her people's lust for conquest, her heavy industries, her general staff. She kept her shipyards, her research laboratories, her shrewd cartel system. She kept extensive assets abroad, an illusion that she had been betrayed instead of beaten, the know-how and the skilled labor in all the fields essential to war. Upon this foundation, she built for war so skillfully and camouflaged it so well at first that only a few realists, dismissed outside Germany as crackpots or hate mongers, were aware of it. Once the camouflage was thrown aside, the world could hardly believe its eyes. Yet the relentless, almost logical progress of a nation's will to war had been going on for years without a check. Cautious at first but gradually accelerating, Germany moved toward her goal. She seemed invincible until she hit something even stronger—the British spirit of the blitz in 1940; the Russian spirit of Stalingrad and Leningrad in 1942. These were the high-water marks of Germany's sea of blood. How did the waves rise so high in so short a time?

The preparation for 1939 began even before the armistice of 1918. That summer the military leaders knew they were beaten, at least for the time being. To Ludendorff, the strategist of German headquarters, August 8 was the "black day" of the German Army, although the Allied generals were grimly preparing for a campaign of 1919 and even 1920. It was the German high command that engineered the "revolution" which sent the Kaiser into exile and brought forward a group of unhappy civilians to take the odium of surrender. The high command never loosed its grip on the strings that controlled this and the succeeding puppet governments of republican Germany.

Before the Versailles Treaty was ratified in 1920, the German generals had thought of and put into execution a device for evading the hundred thousand men limitation placed on their army. They recruited "police" who lived in barracks, drilled like soldiers and wore military uniforms. The Allies protested, so the Germans, still cautious, changed the name of this special force. They did not change its character. Nor did they do anything to discourage wholly illegal military organizations which kept alive the warlike spirit of youth.

Within another year, Germany was finding means to avoid two other consequences of her defeat. By May 10, 1921, she had succeeded in getting her reparations bill cut from \$56.5 billion to \$33 billion. Thirteen days later, the German Supreme Court at Leipzig began a farce—solemnly dubbed a trial. It was the German idea of a substitute for the court martial of men against whom an Allied commission had compiled "the most striking list of crimes that has ever been drawn up to the shame of those who committed them"—the description is that of the commission. The German government professed to be helpless. It said it could not arrest these individuals for delivery to Allied justice but it could try them at home. The Allies agreed to a test case of twelve obscure men who were raised to the status of popular heroes in Germany because they were permitted to be portrayed as martyrs rather than criminals. They were not put to the inconvenience of martyrdom, however, for six were acquitted altogether. The others received trifling sentences worthy of a rather serious traffic violation, and two of them were permitted to escape before their terms were up. That ended the "punishment" of war criminals. No more were brought to trial by Germany; the Allies did not press their authority under the treaty to do the job themselves.

Meanwhile, the conversion of German industry to peace (and to a more modern war technique) was proceeding rapidly. The latest types of furnaces replaced some rather old-fashioned steel mills that had been good enough for World War I but would not do in World War II. While European industry was struggling to complete reconversion to peace—much of it had to be rebuilt because of German destruction—Germany reached her prewar industrial output by 1922. Krupp and Thyssen converted their heavy gun factories—the weapons they could make were obsolete anyway—and concentrated on building up their modern plants for peace. These could be producing steel for war just as well at any time. The shipyards turned from submarines to merchant vessels, which soon were competing to advantage with the older, slower ships surrendered to the Allies. The chemical industries regained their place in world cartels. And everywhere research into new war weapons and the techniques for making them was carried on in secret or camouflaged laboratories. A hidden general staff co-ordinated the work of these recruits of industry with the regular army's hundred thousand men who were being trained as a nucleus of specialists. Around them a mass machine would one day be assembled. It would then take in the hundreds of thousands of Germans who drilled enthusiastically in sports clubs and longed for the day of real military training, the airplane pilots who were being trained abroad, the German-owned industries established outside the Reich to produce military instruments which the Allies had forbidden in Germany.

One of the supposed reasons for the speed-up of German industry and trade was the need to export in order to meet reparations payments. A great part of these was expected to come from a tax on exports. But although Germany's production was growing, the reparations schedules were so far from met that in the whole course of the struggle to collect, Germany actually paid out less than half as much as she received in foreign loans which were never repaid. By 1924, the Allies had tried in turn friendly negotiations, threats and the actual occupation of the Ruhr by French and Belgian armies. Each attempt added to the perplexities of the reparations problem which baffled the experts. But the result of every procedure was simple. None of them worked.

More was expected of the Dawes plan of August, 1924, drawn up by a committee of specialists headed by the Chicago banker and future Vice President. This program assigned specific German revenues to reparations and established Allied commissions and an agent general in Berlin to supervise their collection. But these officials had no authority to interfere with German trade or finance, public or private—a committee of Allied jurists that year offered a formal opinion that any such interference would be illegal.

Not all Germany's preparations could be kept secret, even in this earliest stage of the Reich's march along "the road back." Under the treaty, one of the three occupied Rhineland zones was to be evacuated in 1925 if Germany had lived up to her obligations. On January 5, the Allied governments sent a note to Berlin declaring the zone would not be evacuated because of these specific treaty violations:

1. Failure to demilitarize factories
2. Reconstitution of the general staff
3. Enlistment of short-term recruits
4. Failure to reorganize the police
5. Retention of surplus property

The most serious of these defaults was the first. Trained soldiers and clever strategists are not so dangerous if they have no equipment. But the existence of a powerful industrial machine lent strength to each of the other potential war forces in Germany.

Instead of dealing with the factories which were not

demilitarized, the Allies staged one of those full dress international conferences which did so much between wars for the business of selected resorts and so little for the peace of the world. This one was held at Locarno in October, 1925. It was supposed to settle forever the then boundaries of Germany on the west—but not the east—and to be a triumph of co-operation because Germany was treated as an equal. A month later, still under the influence of what was called admiringly the Locarno spirit, the Allies began evacuting the first Rhineland zone.

The next year Germany entered the League of Nations, where her chief role was to disrupt disarmament discussions by arguing for equality of armaments. It became plain that Germany did not want the world disarmed if it included herself; she wanted the right to build her armies up to the level of any others.

Actually, she already was the strongest power in Europe. Her strength was in steel and coal, chemicals and synthetics, electric power and light metals—the real sinews of modern war. But in December, 1926, the Allies declared themselves satisfied with German disarmament, and on January 31, 1927, the Inter-Allied Commissions of Control were withdrawn. The only vestige of supervision over Germany was that exercised by the commissions watching reparations. Even this came to an end when the Dawes plan was replaced in June, 1929, by one named after Owen D. Young. Besides scaling down the German debt still further, the Young plan abolished the watching commissions. Probably they were quite useless since they were without authority to do more than report. But their departure removed the last remnant of Allied control over

German economy, even in theory. Then on June 30, 1930, the last Allied troops left Germany, too, five years ahead of the time fixed eleven years before in the Versailles Treaty.

The pace of German rearmament was faster after that. For several years the leaders of industry had been giving increasing support to the Nazis. Attacks upon the republic grew more open and frequent, and as the depression deepened everywhere Hitler, whose attraction for a people bent on war could never be understood by peaceful nations, came to power. That day, January 30, 1933, served notice on the world that Germany was committed to conquest. The last traces of freedom were being stamped out under Nazi boots; the last few Germans who dared to talk of peace and mean it were fleeing into exile or dying behind the barbed wire of concentration camps. Germany was strong enough to assume the offensive. It came at first in the form of the world-wide propaganda of Pan-Germanism, in demands for colonies and boundary "rectification," in fierce economic aggression which brought smaller states into the German trade orbit, in an almost open campaign of stockpiling and industrial development. Within six months the course was so plain that Douglas Miller, United States commercial attaché in Berlin, wrote on August 1, 1933, to his superiors that the Reich's Assistant Secretary of Commerce Feder had expressed privately the real Nazi aims. The first two were:

1. Breaking the Versailles Treaty
2. Restoring Germany's military superiority

Faster and faster the Third Reich sped down the road to war. The milestones flashed by. January 13, 1935—*Saar plebiscite.* (Coal and a busy hive of factories came under the swastika that day, as in accordance with the treaty, the people of the basin voted whether to return to Germany, become French or remain under League of Nations control.) March 16, 1935—*Conscription.* (Starting off with one year's military training for every male youth, in August the term was raised to two years. Feder's first point had been realized; the second was on its way to reality.) June 18, 1935—*German Navy reborn.* (A treaty with Great Britain authorized the Reich to build warships, even including submarines, up to 35 per cent of British tonnage. It was the same ratio that France with all her colonies had enjoyed under previous naval limitation treaties.) March 7, 1936—*Rhineland reoccupied.* (Without any opposition the new German Army marched into the district which by treaty was to be forever demilitarized, and soon the Siegfried Line, before whose guns American boys were to die by thousands, was being traced along the border.) September 9, 1936—*Four Year Plan.* (This was designed to make Germany self-sufficient in the raw materials of war. When it was completed—and if it could be done in three years instead of four, the Germans liked it better—the Reich would be ready to strike.) November 25, 1936—*Rome-Berlin-Tokyo Axis.* (This particular date marked the signing of the German-Japanese treaty. The Axis was completed by the signature of Italy a little later.) July 24, 1937—*Industrial "draft."* (The formation this day of the Hermann Goering trust, which was to swarm over all German war industry, was the signal that factories were being mobilized.) March 13, 1938—*Anschluss.* (As the Nazi terror struck Austria, as a new crop of exiles and martyrs was harvested, the world began to believe Hitler really meant what he had been saying, but the German race toward war had gone into its final sprint now.) September 29, 1938—*Munich.* (The name was to become a shameful synonym for appeasement. The date was the twentieth anniversary of a conversation in which Hindenburg and Ludendorff told the Kaiser that the jig was up this time, that he would have to ask for peace.) March 15, 1939—*Prague taken.* March 22, 1939—*Memel annexed.* April 28, 1939—*Polish treaty denounced; British naval treaty denounced.* August 23, 1939—*Russo-German pact.* September 1, 1939—*WAR.*

Somewhere in Germany, fanatical young corporals—perhaps even privates and sergeants, too—are weeping as bitterly as Hitler did in 1918. Soon, like him, they will be dreaming of another chance at world conquest and reminding each other in beer halls and shabby eating places how narrowly they missed success this time. They will get that chance if the United Nations merely repeat the controls that proved so ineffective before. For the industrial leaders of Germany already are laying their plans. They did not even wait for final defeat in World War II before beginning to mobilize for World War III. This is not a guess based on past performances. It is a proved and documented fact. One of the documents is a report of a meeting in Strasbourg as long ago as August 10, 1944, of the principal German industrialists with interests in France. It was supplied to our own army by a Frenchman who attended and for whose reliability military intelligence can vouch. It was submitted by the

Office of Assistant Chief of Staff, G-2, of Supreme Headquarters Allied Expeditionary Force.

At the Hotel Rotes Haus that day gathered the representatives of Krupp, Roehling, Messerschmitt, Rheinmetall, Hecho, Bussing and Volkswagenwerk—an imposing segment of German heavy industry. Also present were engineers from big factories in Posen. Also officials of the naval and armaments ministries. Dr. Scheid, who held high rank in the Nazi SS organization besides being director of Hecho, presided. He advised the others that "German industry must realize that the war cannot be won and that it must take steps in preparation for a postwar commercial campaign." The steps were to be alliances with foreign firms, as individuals so as to allay suspicion, and groundwork for big foreign credits to Germany. The report adds:

> As examples of the kind of penetration which had been most useful in the past, Dr. Scheid cited the fact that patents for stainless steel belonged to the Chemical Foundation, Inc., New York, and the Krupp Company of Germany jointly and that the U.S. Steel Corporation, Carnegie Illinois, American Steel and Wire, National Tube, etc., were thereby under obligation to work with the Krupp concern. He also cited the Zeiss Company, the Leica Company and the Hamburg-American Line as firms which had been especially effective in protecting German interests abroad and gave their New York addresses to the industrialists at this meeting.

A more select session for the representatives of Krupp, Hecho and Roehling followed. Apparently its main purpose was to permit the Armaments Ministry official to inform them that they must be prepared to finance the

Nazi party as an underground movement after defeat, in emulation of the French Maquis. The industrialists were told to follow this program:

First, secure ample funds abroad, for which purpose the Nazis were relaxing rules against exporting capital. These funds are to be at the disposal of the Nazis in their underground campaign, (but the industrialists will be repaid by concessions and orders when the party comes back to power.) Two Swiss banks through which operations may be conducted were named, and the possibility of acquiring a Swiss dummy at a cost of 5 per cent was noted.

Second, each of the big German factories was to create a small research bureau that had no ostensible connection with the main plant. They were to be hidden in the cities or camouflaged in villages near water-power sites under the guise of studying hydroelectric resources. All plans, drawings and documents needed to continue research into new weapons of war were to be turned over to the bureaus but, they "must not be allowed to fall into the hands of the enemy." Each bureau also was to have its liaison agent with the Nazis.

Third, while the Nazis recognize "that certain of its best known leaders will be condemned as war criminals," the industrialists are to find safe places in the research bureaus for "less conspicuous but most important members."

In the face of such planning, the road to war could not be blocked by the kind of controls the Allies imposed last time, even if more rigorously applied. In the light of history and what we know of German plans for writing another chapter of history, we could look forward to this sort of a program:

1. Destruction of all German weapons and military installations. But they would be obsolete before the Germans would want them anyway.

2. Confiscation of the German merchant fleet. That virtually compels the Germans to build newer, faster and better ships which can enjoy a competitive advantage on important trade routes.

3. War factories to be dismantled or converted to peacetime production. The United States has demonstrated with what speed these factories can be converted back again and how much basic production is the same for peace or war.

4. Control commissions to watch for a period of years to see that no munitions are made. But the United Nations would get tired of watching and in any case, the factories would be ready for conversion as soon as the term of years expired.

5. Restitution of loot. It is unlikely that much of it can be identified, but it would hardly slake the German thirst for more loot later.

6. Reparations for the devastated countries in actual materials rather than money over a period of years. This sounds just, but it could further strengthen German industry and tend to weaken the industry of the recipients.

7. Allied control commissions to supervise German economy in the interest of collecting reparations. Measures to be taken would be a fruitful source of inter-Allied disputes and would saddle the Allies with responsibility for the German economy.

8. War criminals to be tried by an international tribunal under democratic court procedures. Germany would reap a crop of martyrs, for the trials would be a sounding board for Nazi dogma.

9. Nazi party and all its affiliates to be disbanded. But no one could prevent new organizations underground.

10. A democratic form of government to be given to Germany. However, by its very nature democracy cannot be given; it must be worked for by any people who achieve it. Furthermore, the imposition of a democratic *form* of government would saddle it with the blame for inevitable German hardships and make the very idea of democracy even more distasteful to Germans than it is now.

11. Germany's foreign assets to be turned over to this government and their use controlled by the Allies. That brings Germany back into participation in cartels or any other international business organizations and offers her a chance at new economic aggression.

12. Re-education of the German people by the United Nations. What educator would undertake to find the number of qualified teachers needed? What educator would make the unqualified statement that any foreign education can be imposed successfully upon sixty million people?

13. Occupation of Germany by Allied troops, especially Americans, for a period of years. If the troops stay long enough, they tend to absorb sympathy for the occupied territory or even the ideas of the people among whom they live. The memory of injury fades, and the desire of men to go home is always strong, so that probably the

occupation would become more relaxed and finally end ahead of time, just as it did before.

14. Cession of important areas to neighboring countries and perhaps even partition of the balance. Well, we learned once how rapidly ceded areas can be taken back, along with more than the original loss, once a rearmed Germany is on the march.

On those fourteen points, pessimism is justified. But fortunately there are other points. The wisdom and ingenuity of peaceful men in dealing with Germany was not exhausted between 1918 and 1939. There are ways of attaining the objectives for which we have fought, provided the objectives are not lost to view in a fog compounded of the mists of sentimentality and the soot of "practical diplomacy." Peace is our goal, peace in which the wonders of the modern world can be put to the service of man instead of to his destruction. For the first time in human history we know enough and are skillful enough to feed and clothe and house all the people of this earth. There can even be something over for fun and comforts and health. Only if we have peace, though, will these remain possibilities.

So, first things first. Before we can go forward to fulfill the promise of peace, the threat of war must be taken away from our backs. In our time, Germany has been the chief nation to make that threat seriously—with Japan a close second, of course—and Germany has put it into execution twice. A third time may well be fatal to civilization.

Chapter II

A PATH TO PEACE

MY OWN PROGRAM FOR ENDING THE menace of German aggression consists, in its simplest terms, of depriving Germany of all heavy industries. The reason for selecting heavy industries is that with them Germany can quickly and terribly convert once more to war. Without them, no matter how savage her aggressive aims may be, she cannot make war.

For longer than living men can remember, the greatest threat to peace anywhere in the world has been Germany's lust for armed conquest. Even more than the German Army, that lust has found its release through German heavy industry. It was done in two ways, both of which will be not only possible but probable again if we permit Germany to retain the basic means of aggression.

First, of course, was the actual manufacture of the weapons of modern war. The guns, planes, tanks, submarines which a Germany with heavy industry could produce fifteen or twenty years from now would be as far beyond present weapons as ours today are beyond those of 1917. We had just a taste of that future in the jet planes and buzz bombs of last year. If Germany keeps the means to perfect such weapons, she will use them.

The second role of heavy industry in the German plan of aggression was and will be economic blitzkrieg. This can be and has been as demoralizing as the military article. The heavy hand of German power was laid upon the economy of her neighbors—and throughout Europe industries withered, scarcity grew, fear multiplied.

Any country's war potential these days can be measured by its heavy industries much more accurately than by the size of its army, navy and air force at any given moment. In four years the peacetime industrial machine of the United States was converted into a weapon that dwarfed Germany's once famous Luftwaffe, Wehrmacht and the rest. That fact, however, only lends point and emphasis to the equally pertinent fact that Germany's industrial machine in not much more time was converted into a weapon that crushed the proud French Army theoretically safe behind its Maginot Line. Soldiers understand this very well. For every big air raid on a fortress or any army camp that we used to read about in the newspapers, we saw accounts of hundreds directed against important industrial centers. The Allied high command knew where Germany's real strength lay, and pounded at production accordingly.

That being so, it would seem rather obvious that to disarm Germany in any real sense of the word is to remove the industries that would make rearmament possible. It is all very well to confiscate guns, planes, tanks, submarines, military installations and so on. It is even more important to remove or destroy the German plants where new and more horrifying weapons of war could be forged. It is most important of all to keep those plants from being rebuilt.

Germany's real armament is a triple threat of metallurgical, chemical and electrical industries. The prewar Reich dominated Europe in those fields. Therefore, she dominated Europe militarily as well, until she challenged even greater industrial powers. Without these factories, the Germans could not have indulged their lust for conquest in 1914 or 1939. Without these factories, they could not do it again. The specific factories which will always be a threat to peace in German hands are:

1. *The Metals Group.* Blast furnaces, open hearths, blooming mills, forges, rolling mills—all the plants used in turning iron ore into finished primary iron and steel products—operate exactly the same for war as for peace. To carry through disarmament of Germany in this area, she must be deprived not only of these basic establishments but also of all factories capable of making machine tools, airplane engines, airplanes, locomotives and other heavy railroad equipment, Diesel engines, steel rails, heavy tractors, automobiles. They can be converted to war too fast for our safety.

2. *The Chemical Group.* These plants are the source of Germany's explosives, rubber, gasoline. They were so important a weapon that their development and operation were largely supervised by the Army, even before the advent of the Nazis. In removing all heavy chemical factories from the Reich, it would be necessary to deprive her of her position in international cartels in this field. The production of such items as phamaceuticals might be permitted, as it can be carried on in small units which need not become a danger. However, the items permitted must be carefully selected, bearing in mind that a perfume factory, for example, can turn to the manufacture of poison gas without any conversion problem at all.

3. *The Electrical Group.* It is more than a coincidence that "power" has become a synonym for electricity. Of that kind of power Germany should be permitted to retain only so much as she needs for her household and reduced industrial needs. The tremendous loads that produced aluminum and magnesium would be unnecessary for her, since she would not be permitted to retain any machinery to make the light metals which can so easily be fabricated into planes. Nor would she be allowed plants for the manufacture of dynamos, turbines, communications devices or electronic equipment. Factories capable of producing electrical goods no more deadly than toasters, vacuum cleaners and hair curlers, would be left.

In de-industrializing Germany, the factories taken from her would be rebuilt in other parts of Europe. They would constitute some reparation for damage done, but they would also help balance Europe better industrially so that the Continent need never again be overshadowed by the machine power of a single nation. Devastated countries should have priority in claiming Germany's industrial equipment.

Until the time of the Potsdam Conference delay was the chief danger. It was necessary to the success of the program that each country should have a limited time to dismantle and remove what it wanted from Germany. It is now equally important that any heavy industry remaining anywhere in the Reich shall be destroyed immediately.

There have been transfers of industry quite as spectacular and as difficult as this. Germany herself moved a whole group of war industries from her western borders into Silesia and behind the Sudeten mountains in an effort to escape air raids. German war plants in Austria and Moravia operated with heavy machinery looted from France and Poland. Nor has the ability to move heavy industry over the landscape been a German monopoly. Russia took many plants apart in the face of advancing German armies and put them together again hundreds of miles away in places whose people had hardly known what a factory looked like. America has shipped whole factories overseas as Lend-Lease. China moved hundreds of establishments into the interior on the backs of men, women and children.

Machinery can be moved or broken up for scrap; buildings can be demolished; workers can be sent to other jobs. But coal in the ground is not so easily disposed of. The Ruhr Valley had 70 per cent to 80 per cent of Germany's coal production (not including lignite). Furthermore, Ruhr coal was especially well adapted for coking and therefore for steelmaking. The existence of this coal was the reason why the Ruhr became the greatest single industrial center in Europe. And coal is the foundation, too, of a great deal of Germany's electrical and chemical progress. It would probably be the magnet drawing to itself any future German effort to re-establish heavy industry. Even after the removal of all Ruhr factories that escaped destruction in the war, the mines would remain a potential source of German rearmament.

The coal cannot be taken away from the Ruhr (except by the trainload as it is mined), so the Ruhr should be taken away from Germany. Annexed to any other country, it would be a perpetual storm center, but it could safely

THE RUHR VALLEY

be placed under the control of a governing body established by the United Nations.

The exact form and personnel of this commission may well be left to the Allied leaders. The extent of its authority is more important. As the government of the Ruhr, it would become the legal owner of the coal fields in perpetuity. It would exercise police powers and all other administrative functions. Its first obligation would be to see that no Ruhr coal is ever used to set up new heavy industries, whether within the valley or in some other part of Germany. The second responsibility would be the use of Ruhr coal for the benefit of European reconstruction and development generally.

Of course, no German should sit on the Ruhr's governing commission. In fact, no Germans should be left in the Ruhr at all. Their presence would lead to a repetition of the difficulties encountered in the Saar after World War I. The Ruhr must not be tied around the neck of the world security organization, as the Saar was bound to the League of Nations. The promise of a plebiscite after a term of years, which helped disrupt the Saar settlement, would not be necessary in the Ruhr. The people would not be under alien rule because they would not be there. Their places would be taken by French, Belgian, Dutch and other workers.

The exodus from the Ruhr which was caused by Allied bombing was a more difficult experience for the Germans than their transfer in time of peace. It is unfortunate that so many of them were permitted to return. But the world cannot afford to have such a dangerous weapon as the Ruhr in German hands. The miners, factory hands, transportation and service workers—the whole German population—would be contributing their bit to a sound European settlement if they were sent back to seek their livelihood in the farms and shops of a de-industrialized Reich. Most of them probably would become workers on the land, and as such a far less potent force for war than they have been these last two generations.

As helpful to the cause of peace as the removal of these workers will be the passing of the German heavy industrialist. In the past, the steel, chemical and electrical tycoons have been the most persistent allies of the militarists. With the destruction of their factories in the Reich, they will lose power.

One other loophole for German heavy industry and future German aggression remains. That is the German-controlled factory abroad, linked to the network of German foreign trade. Steel mills in Sweden, machine tool plants in Switzerland, a chemical industry in Argentina might serve a new set of German war lords almost as well as the Krupp Works at Essen. This is no fanciful fear conjured out of a fevered imagination. It is a very real threat and one which the Germans brought into reality with deadly effect in the past. The United States Senate's Kilgore Committee, after a careful study of this whole problem reported that after World War I:

> . . . The firm of Carl Zeiss, by creating a manufacturing subsidiary in Holland, was able to evade the prohibition on the manufacture of military optical instruments, such as range-finders and periscopes. The firm of Friedrich Krupp nullified a restriction on the manufacture of armaments by gaining control of Bofors, a Swedish armament firm.

The same pattern developed in the closing months of the war, as the Nazis recognized the inevitable. The meeting of the German industrialists in Strasbourg's Hotel Rotes Haus in August, 1944, was only one example. Enough others were brought before the Kilgore Committee to inspire the charge:

> The German aggressors have begun to pursue a strategy which they found successful a quarter century ago; they are already deploying their economic reserves throughout the world in preparation for a third attempt at world domination. They plan to resume the old commercial pattern which served them so well. We must insure that in the defeat of Germany the economic forces of aggression will be forever eliminated along with the military forces.

A practical program for carrying out this Senatorial recommendation would have to include:

1. Seizure and disposition of German assets abroad.
2. Prohibition of German investment in foreign countries.
3. Strict United Nations control of all German credits obtained by exports, by inheritance or in any other way.
4. Similar control over all German foreign exchange operations.
5. Prohibition of German participation in international cartels. (This is apart from any other solution of the cartel question.)
6. Elimination of German ownership of property in neutral countries.

Under the Nazis, German business assets abroad never were considered as the private property of their owners but as a weapon of economic aggression, political intervention or military preparation for the German state. The state decided just what business its citizen might keep abroad. Then the state told him what to do with it. One group would be kept operating at enormous loss (met by domestic subsidies) to draw a foreign nation's economy or part of it under German influence. Another would be commanded to use its funds for propaganda, espionage, sabotage, bribery or some other form of political penetration. Still another would be the medium for stockpiling materials needed in the coming war—oil, rubber, nickel, tungsten, etc.

The effect of this was so obviously dangerous that six months before Pearl Harbor, on my recommendation to President Roosevelt, the Treasury "froze" all German assets in this country. Most of the other American republics followed our example for their own protection from the Nazis. If these Germans could create so much disturbance in a more powerful country an ocean away from the center of Nazi infection, it is plain with what devastating effect their trading ethics and assets could be used upon relatively helpless nations within easy bomber range. Confiscation of these assets—with the owners compensated in marks by Germany—would prevent their use for a German campaign of revenge. Distributed among nations despoiled by Germany, the property would constitute partial compensation for damage suffered.

As it is not enough to destroy German war industry without making sure it cannot be rebuilt, so the possible renewal of German economic aggression must be blocked at the source after the current assets are confiscated. Outright ownership could be replaced by the control of a dominant trader, which would permit the Reich to attempt once more the purchase of military supplies and of men's consciences.

One preventive measure is Allied control over all German foreign exchange transactions. The Germans perfected the use of such control as an instrument for war. Funds for foreign purchases were allocated to items that would help the German war effort. They ordered profits used to buy war supplies or propaganda or a shipload of butter. The same controls may be used to make Germany's foreign trade an instrument for peace. It would at least enable the Allies to be certain that a tractor ostensibly meant for farm use does not have a motor powerful enough to haul the biggest type of field gun.

Exclusion of Germany from cartels is an obvious lesson of experience. As one specific example, the production of magnesium in the United States was limited by cartel agreements so that even under the spur of the defense emergency our output had gone up from 2,500 tons to only 5,680 while the Germans were turning out 19,000 tons. It was this sort of thing which prompted the Kilgore Committee to declare:

> Almost immediately, as a consequence of this unholy alliance between Hitler and the cartelists, Germany's plans for economic warfare, aimed at ultimate world domination, were expanded. The German Government became a silent partner in the multitude of cartel agreements among German, American, British, French and other concerns with which German industry had established cartel relations.
>
> Under cover of cartel agreements, Germany pene-

trated the economy of other nations, including the United States. Using their cartel affiliates or subsidiaries, German industrialists built up a network which impaired the production of other nations, obtained sources of foreign exchange for Germany, gathered economic intelligence and spread Nazi propaganda.

The argument against attempting to control another nation's economy down to the last detail is that even with whole armies of inspectors and technicians it is almost impossible, as the Nazis found in the countries they occupied. Applied to the internal economy of Germany, this is a sound argument. But foreign trade is another matter. It can be controlled by a few key people in a few key places. The two problems are as different as collecting a nation's internal revenue and collecting the customs. The United States needs fifty thousand persons for the first task; the second is efficiently performed by eight thousand.

The elimination of German heavy industry is no hate campaign. The world has seen enough of hatred, and the United Nations have no need to adopt the policy of their enemies. Nor is the program a panacea for peace. It is, however, an essential preliminary to peace, to realization of the ideals for which the United States has fought, to the security of all nations (even including Germany), and to that better world which the sacrifices of all peoples have entitled them to expect.

What to do with Germany is still the first of the big postwar questions the United Nations must answer. The right answer will give us a tremendous lift toward the attainment of our other aims—toward what Woodrow Wilson called a "community of power" to replace the balance of power and keep the peace, toward the increasing exchange of goods and ideas among nations, toward the continuance of full production and full employment at home.

Chapter III

A STRONG EUROPE IS BETTER THAN A STRONG GERMANY

THE END OF GERMAN HEAVY INDUSTRY will do more than relieve the world of an intolerable fear of renewed aggression. It will relieve all Europe of the iron bonds which were made in Germany to confine the industries of the rest of the Continent within small, unnatural limits. Once set free from German chains, European industry in general will soon far more than replace the production taken from the Reich. The net result will be more steel, chemicals, electrical equipment, more jobs and fatter payrolls, in short, a rising standard of living for all the people in Europe, not just sixty million Germans.

The notion that German heavy industry is indispensable to the well-being of Europe is a myth sedulously nurtured by German propaganda over many years. Among those who are trying to keep it alive today are the men who did business with the German cartels in the past, to the profit of themselves and the ruin or near ruin of their own countries.

But examined in the light of prewar facts and postwar probabilities, the theory breaks down at every point. In its place are the realities, which prove:

1. That Germany filled a relatively small proportion of Europe's needs.
2. That these needs could readily be supplied by other nations.
3. That if efficiency and common sense had been the only factors, other nations would have been supplying them long since. They were hampered by ruthless German trade practices.
4. That Germany absorbed a relatively small amount of Europe's (and the world's) exports.
5. That her suppliers will find even larger markets when the industry of the Continent is better balanced than it can be under German domination.
6. That Germany herself can achieve a fair level of prosperity without heavy industry.
7. That removal of German heavy industry will help develop the industries of other nations and result in a higher standard of living for Europe, making her a better market for (and neighbor to) all the rest of the world.

The advocates of a Germany strong in heavy industry usually assert that such a menacing colossus is necessary to "European economy" or at least to the maintenance of "economic equilibrium in Europe." Actually there is no "European economy," certainly not in the sense that there is a United States economy. Some thirty countries in Europe have their separate economies, and a great variety of them, too. As for "economic equilibrium in Europe," it has been upset a great deal more than it has been stabilized by German industry and its overlords.

In point of fact, Germany never did supply Europe with very much iron and steel, metallurgical products, chemicals or electrical equipment—the chief items to be forbidden

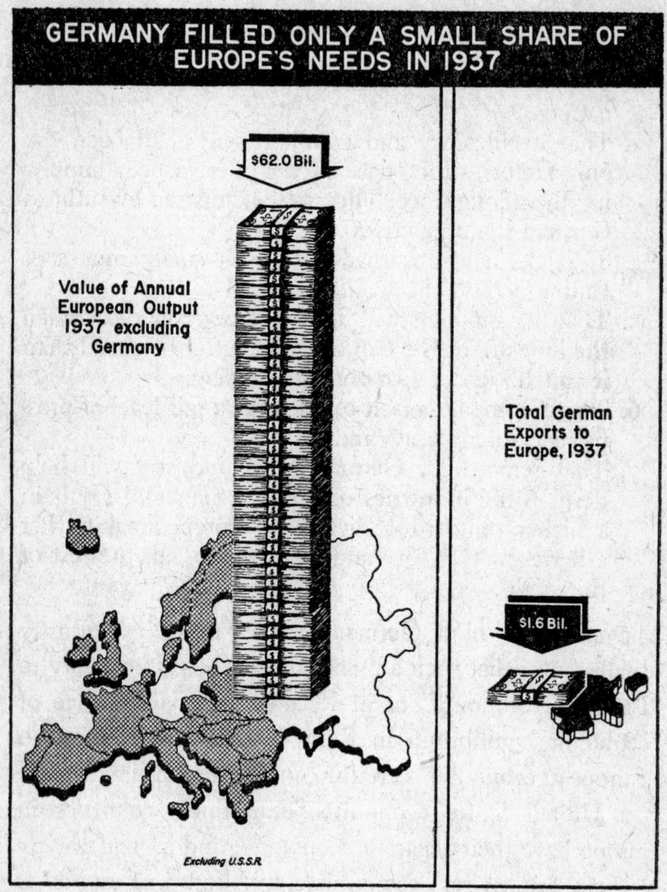

her. In her best years of exports, 1929 and 1937, she sold $775,000,000 worth of these products to all the countries of Europe put together. Europe's total imports (excluding Germany) were $13,100,000,000 in 1937 and Germany supplied $1,600,000,000.

A STRONG EUROPE IS BETTER

Even Germany's 12.2 per cent of the European market was achieved by lavish use of those trade practices which the world hopes to abolish in the interest of peace and prosperity. Even before 1933, Germany gave government subsidies to stimulate exports. After Hitler came to power the subsidies rose to fantastic heights. Clearing arrangements, multiple currency maneuvers and foreign exchange discrimination were used as part of a system to force other countries to buy in Germany. If they refused, they lost the German market for their own products.

Under any kind of fair competition, Germany would be lucky after the war, even if her factories could be rebuilt and reconverted quickly, to reach much more than half her prewar exports of the products of heavy industries. Perhaps $400,000,000 worth could be disposed of without violent artificial aids. In the proportion of exports in Germany's most successful years this would be divided:

Iron, steel and other metal products	$ 72,000,000
Machinery (except electrical)	100,000,000
Electrical equipment	48,000,000
Chemicals	48,000,000
Automobiles	32,000,000

The idea that these amounts could not be supplied by plants which will be established outside Germany and by existing industries in Europe is fantastic. But even if Europe could not fill the gap, the British and Americans, who have greatly increased their plant capacity during the war, could easily serve this market. The whole amount is about 4 per cent of the minimum estimates of postwar United States exports under full production.

It is impossible to measure statistically just how much

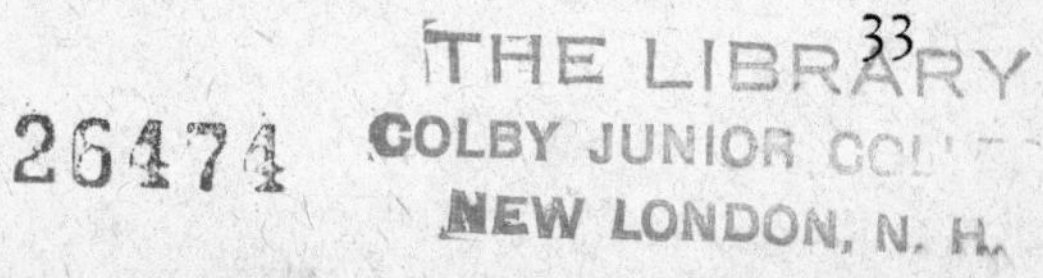

German oppression prevented the normal, natural industrialization of other European countries. Cartels were the chief weapon, reinforced by export subsidies, special kinds of currencies and clearing agreements.

Clearing agreements were bilateral arrangements ostensibly designed to prevent exchange fluctuations. They did it by carrying on trade between the two countries at an agreed rate of exchange without either using the currency of the other. Each set up a clearing office. Importers paid to this clearing office in their own currency. Exporters were paid by the clearing office, also in their own currency. In the long run the amounts had to balance as between imports and exports and as between the two countries. A typical transaction between Germany and Poland would work out like this:

A Pole sells a German a trainload of timber. The Polish clearing office pays its citizens in zlotys; the German timber buyer pays his clearing office in marks. In order to get its money back, the Polish clearing office has to be sure a Pole buys something in Germany of the same value as the timber—automobiles perhaps. When the Polish dealer buys German cars, he pays zlotys into his own clearing office; the German clearing office pays the German car manufacturer off in marks.

It sounds like good business until one of two things happens—maybe both. Germany fears Poland may be motorizing her army with the automobiles or getting too strong with German steel and insists that Poland take harmonicas or Christmas tree decorations. Or the Polish dealer may prefer to buy American cars because they stand up better under Polish road conditions.

Either case weakens Poland and usually in a vital industrial point. She takes harmonicas instead of building up her industry because she has the money standing to her credit in Germany and cannot use it any other way. Or she has to force the Polish dealer to buy German instead of American cars either by a discriminatory tariff, import quotas or exchange controls. Even if Poland wanted to set up automobile plants or machinery factories of her own, she would be hampered by the need for taking German products through the clearing agreement.

Multiple marks achieved the same ends through a different device. Germany would make payments to foreign creditors only in special kinds of marks. While the official rate was 40 cents, there was a travel mark quoted at about 15 cents, good only for tourist travel in Germany. Other types of marks sold at even lower prices. They were expendable only for the purchase of German goods by foreigners who had made special arrangements. This in effect made the German products cheaper. Foreign holders of these marks were tempted strongly to get machinery from the Reich instead of from their own manufacturers or from another country which did not offer this bribe of bargain-basement currencies.

Export subsidies achieved the identical purpose. Part of a special tax placed on all German industries was used to subsidize exporters, who could then undersell any local manufacturer in Europe in his own market. The German could either drive competitors out of business or force them into agreements to restrict their output. In either case, European industry in general was stunted in its natural growth.

But the really big thing was the international cartel, through which the power of other nations to defend themselves was weakened. The United States was not immune. Because Germans could force even United States aluminum, optical goods and chemical giants to restrict their volume, territories, prices and new products, the German Army felt itself able to make its bid for world conquest.

Powerful as we are, the Germans succeeded in imposing upon us, through the medium of our own international industrialists, restrictions on the production of vital war materials. Before we could get rid of the deadening effect of the German control in our own back yard, we had lost months at a stage of the war when seconds were costing lives. For those were the months when the Japanese were sweeping to the shores of Australia, the months when the Germans drove to Stalingrad, the months in which Rommel pushed his desert armies almost to Alexandria.

Germans dominated the cartels and used them for war, not because they were wiser or stronger or wealthier but because they concentrated on building for aggression. German members, who virtually had their government as a silent senior partner, were mainly bent on carrying out that government's aggressive policies. Other nationalities joined the cartels for strictly business reasons. The German was linked with his government in a campaign of economic conquest. The American, at the other extreme, was frequently defying his government and in any case concerned solely with the cartel as a means of making money or consolidating industrial power. Therefore the German had a clear field for deploying industry as an auxiliary of the Army. Their colleagues in other countries were usually satisfied with profits, freedom from competition at home and at most a share of foreign markets on a comfortably arranged basis to keep prices up.

The word "cartel" is used rather indiscriminately, often merely as a term of abuse. Strictly speaking, it is an organization by which producers in a given line combine to carry out a common policy of production, prices or sales. It is frequently meant to apply only to an arrangement by which producers restrict their output. In either case, the members retain individual identity although the cartel sets production quotas and prices, divides exclusive territories and sometimes even operates branch plants and sales offices for all members jointly.

For the most part, cartel agreements are illegal in the United States. In Germany they are not only legal but since 1933 compulsory in many instances. They have been rigidly controlled and supervised, as was all business, by the Ministry of Economic Affairs, so the government really directs their policies. Between the world wars, some two or three thousand cartels were organized in Germany. More than one hundred operated on an international scale. These are the ones that carried on Germany's prewar economic hostilities. The extent of their operations can be seen from a Treasury compilation of German subsidiaries and affiliates in just six countries—Turkey, Argentina and the European neutrals Portugal, Spain, Sweden and Switzerland. The list, mostly firms controlled by German cartels, contains 750 names.

Just how Germany's economic aggression against the people of the United States was carried on has been brought to light in this war. Much of it has been discovered by the Treasury Department through our taking over such German outfits in this country as General Aniline & Film and Bosch Magneto. We found that no matter where the heart of the cartel octopus was—in Germany or England or Holland or the United States—the result was the same. The tentacles reached out into all countries,

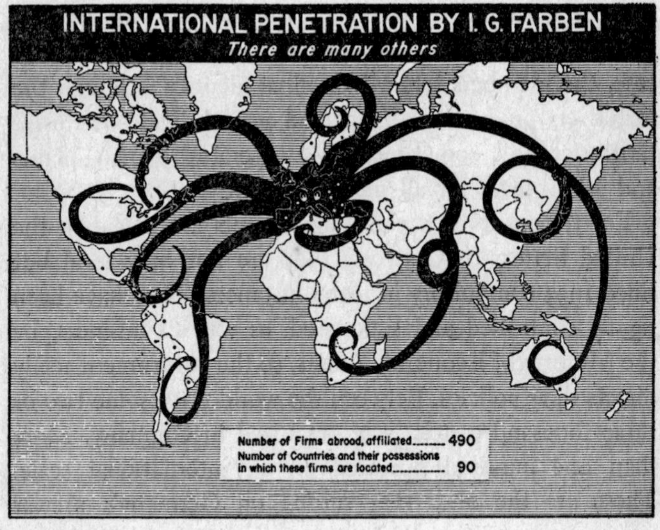

squeezing the natural, beneficial growth of industry and commerce, crushing the independent manufacturer, the small trader, the truly competitive businesses which are the life of commercial and industrial progress.

The German domination of cartels was a menace and worse in more ways than one, but nowhere as much as in keeping other countries from a natural, healthy industrial growth. Germans did it by restrictive agreements within the cartels, by selling at a loss to prevent a new competitor from getting started, by control of patents—often the patents of Americans—and by simple boycott. The result was always a swollen German, and a shrunken world, industry.

The firm of Friedrich Krupp of Essen presents a clear warning as to how German heavy industry would rebuild for war if we allowed it to exist. After World War I, Krupp was required to destroy machinery of war. But a $9,000,000 loan from the United States in 1924 helped it to regain its old position, which before 1914 had enabled it to force the United States Navy to pay three times as much for armor plate as Europeans paid. After the loan, Krupp was sufficiently recovered to invade the United States. Under the laws of Delaware it organized the Krupp-Nirosta Company to hold and license patents. Some of these patents were for stainless steel, and by pooling with our own steel firms, Krupp was able to exercise a tight control over stainless steel companies here. Not only was production restricted, but Krupp-Nirosta sent reports to Essen giving technical information on American producers and telling how much they were producing. When war broke out in 1939, Krupp-Nirosta (the Krupp part of the name was dropped in January, 1940, and a camouflaged Swiss ownership attempted) tried to put through a plan by which German firms in Latin America could get American supplies to maintain German influence there.

Even when a United States firm tried to escape some of the restrictions imposed by Germany, the system was too strong. The American Bosch Company had a series of agreements with Robert Bosch of Stuttgart, made in 1930. Besides the usual clauses limiting production and market territories, American Bosch had to pay such high royalties to Germany for fuel injection pumps and nozzles that in 1939 it wrote the parent company:

"The production of Diesel engines during the past year has declined greatly.... The fundamental problem affecting the further development of Diesel engines in our country today... is almost entirely one of price."

But Bosch of Stuttgart kept the royalties so high that American manufacturers preferred gasoline engines. By 1941 this so seriously hampered our Navy in its building program that on June 19 it pleaded for a "second source of supply." American Bosch had no right to license any other firm to make the vital fuel injection pumps. It had to ask Germany for permission to give this aid to the American defense program! In 1942 one of the reasons given for the success of the U-boats against our shipping was our hopelessly inadequate Diesel engine production. Germany had barred us from going into large-scale manufacture of an essential anti-submarine aid.

The occupation of Germany has revealed a great many details, suspected but now proved, of how the German heavy industrialists prepared for this war and then, seeing defeat, began preparing for the next. When our troops went into Frankfurt, military government officers headed straight for the main offices of I. G. Farben, greatest of German trusts. The officers got there while shells were still bursting in the area. The Germans had done a very thorough job of mixing up the records. Trash and secret agreements, dead files and important contracts were scattered all over the floors and staircases of six stories. Essential documents had been shipped all over Germany. One official had hidden a ten-inch pile of international dye agreements under an innocent layer of family silver. The military found valuable I. G. Farben papers in beer halls, caves, salt mines and even monasteries.

Out of the documents sorted out from the wastepaper emerged proof of German schemes both past and present. One example is the minutes of a meeting at which on March 17, 1939, the legal brains of I. G. Farben met to safeguard the German trust's assets abroad during the war. In the United States this was to be done by transferring patents to General Aniline & Film. Approval of the German Economies Ministry was obtained, and Farben officials wrote:

"We know from previous experience that our American friends are handicapped in their work for us by the existing links and believe that we must help them in the defense of our interests by carrying out the measures described above which they have recommended to us."

Fortunately, Farben's "American friends" had underestimated the vigilance of the Treasury and other American officials. The Treasury took over General Aniline & Film, and the minutes of the German meeting are chiefly interesting as proving the wisdom of our course and as evidence of a plot that failed. But we should not be in the least complacent. For other plots did not fail.

At a whole series of vital points, American production for war was hampered as it had been for peace by the dominant position of German heavy industry. It happened in optical goods, in synthetic rubber, in tungsten carbide for machine tools, in atabrine to fight malaria, in high octane gas, in the new explosive tetracene, in magnesium and beryllium and plexiglass.

If Germany could fit the industrial powers of the United States into her pattern of world conquest, it is easy to guess how completely she could control nearer and weaker neighbors. But we do not need to guess. We know.

In 1926 an international steel cartel was organized. At the time, Germany produced only 2½ per cent more pig iron than France. The cartel agreement fixed the quota of each member, and each was to pay into a common pool one dollar for every ton it produced. But for every ton produced over the quota, the producer had to pay by way of a fine an extra four dollars a ton. The French very thriftily kept within their quota and even cut production a bit now and then to save the dollar a ton. The Germans, on the other hand, seemed to have gone on a spree. They regularly exceeded their quota and cheerfully paid the fine. In one year it amounted to about $10 million for 2,500,000 tons excess production. But it turned out that the Germans knew what they were doing. After a few years they argued plausibly that their increased capacity was so great that it entitled them to a bigger quota. Their increased capacity—second only to that of the United States by then—gave them the power to beat their European rivals over the head to get what they wanted. Their pig iron quota was raised, and by 1938 German steel production was 23,200,000 tons while France dropped to 6,200,000.

Without the cartel deal, the two countries would normally have developed along about the proportions of 1926. As it was, France sold her iron ore to Germany in greater volume, contented herself with an inadequate steel capacity and relinquished to Germany markets she might easily have kept or gained for herself. Germany could get away with it in part because German cartel members were part owners of all the important steel and chemical companies in Europe.

It was the same steel cartel that showed how an industry can be strangled at birth in a little European country. Shortly before the outbreak of the war, Greece was planning to build steel mills of her own. Germany not only refused to supply any equipment after having gained a predominant place in the Greek economy, but used her influence to keep other members of the cartel from doing so. In a letter from the German Steel Cartel to the international body, appears this paragraph:

"We have left no stone unturned in order by all means to prevent the establishment of an iron industry in Greece."

German cartelists prevented the growth of French dye industries and blocked the establishment of a French synthetic oil industry. French industrialists were permitted to make money, but their country was fatally weakened both in the useful crafts of peace and the grim necessities of war.

Through all this growth of German power—achieved because the German government joined the German cartelists in an unequal economic battle against foreign industries—there grew up a legend that Germany was a huge and essential and irreplaceable market for the raw materials of Europe. Yet the figures show she was even less of a factor as a buyer than as a supplier. Almost no one in Europe will miss her heavy industries as a market.

The year 1937 marked Germany's biggest purchases of industrial raw materials and semimanufactures since the peak of the 1929 boom. The enormous iron and steel, metallurgical, electrical and chemical industries, among them, bought from all Europe a grand total of $160,000,000 worth. This is less than the total of raw materials and semimanufactures imported that year by a single United States industry—automobiles.

Nor were these German purchases a matter of life and death for any single country. Sweden was tops—$50,000,000 of the $160,000,000 total. Eight other European countries shared in it to the extent of more than $5,000,000 each. Eleven others had a small, sometimes a negligible portion.

Nearly half of the $160,000,000 was in iron ore. There can be little doubt that a properly balanced European distribution of industry would easily absorb this iron and more, as well as all the other items formerly sold to Germany. Some will be used at home in new industries and to improve local standards of living. Others will be purchased by European countries which are permitted to develop or expand their industries according to the dictates of free competition.

The loss of heavy industry would decrease German imports of agricultural products, and in value this was always more important to Europe than the buying of German heavy industry. But the net amount of food for Europeans to eat will be bigger than ever, for the rest of Europe will feed itself instead of feeding Germany.

Many of Germany's displaced industrial workers will go on the land and improve the frequently inefficient and archaic German farming methods.

The 1937 imports of agricultural products from Europe were unusually high for Germany and reached a total of $360,000,000—the equivalent of about three per cent of the American people's food bill for that year. Whether Germany keeps heavy industry or not, this standard of imports could not be maintained now and would not be reached for a great many years. For one thing, some of the imported food was taken as part of a plan for making other countries dependent on the Reich. More was stockpiled for war. In neither case was it needed to feed the German people. Even if Germany is permitted to keep heavy industry, she could not produce foreign exchange to buy this food without help. The Allies would have to give up reparations and actually grant Germany a priority for machinery and materials for her export industries ahead of the needs of liberated nations. If we treat our friends fairly, Germany will have little food except what she can raise herself.

This does not mean that the other countries of Europe will not sell food. They may well sell more than ever before. The big suppliers of Germany in 1937 were Denmark to the extent of $50,000,000; the Netherlands, Italy and Rumania with more than $40,000,000 each; Yugoslavia and Hungary, about $35,000,000 each. They accounted for about two-thirds of Germany's agricultural imports from Europe. Yet all of these countries except perhaps Denmark and Holland need food for their own people far more than they need exports. Increased industrialization, which they might be able to achieve when freed from German bondage, would permit Yugoslavs, Rumanians, Hungarians and Italians to eat better. They would find a market for real surplus crops in the factory towns of other countries. Denmark and Holland, particularly the latter, would also have bigger home markets and might find buyers in such countries as France, England, and Czechoslovakia.

Actually, even if Germany ceases to be a purchaser of anything at all, an entirely different group of countries from those who sold most to her would have to make the bigger readjustments. They are countries that are facing pretty staggering readjustments anyway. In 1937, five eastern European countries did rely upon Germany for a very large part of their exports, both food and other materials. Bulgaria sold 43 per cent of her total exports to the Reich; Turkey, 36 per cent; Latvia, 35 per cent; Greece, 31 per cent; Estonia, 30 per cent. The percentages were high; the actual amounts relatively small. A very few industries in these countries would enable them to absorb locally all they sold to Germany. A few more industries in other neighboring countries would enable them to expand their exports over the 1937 figure.

The end of heavy industry in Germany will permit transfer of factories to the very places where they would have been located in the first place if access to raw materials, markets, labor and power had been the really decisive factors in European development. The shift could be all the easier because many German heavy industrial plants have been destroyed in the war. It could have been easier still had our own leaders not permitted a partial revival of these factories. Surely, it would be far more reasonable to rebuild them outside the Reich's borders than within. Holland, for example, should make electrical equipment and metal products instead of being merely a port through which German exports were routed. France should make steel herself from her own iron ore, using German coke as she always has. Britain may find a reviving market for her coal. Chemical industries might spring up all over Europe. The bauxite of southeastern Europe and Danube power give the clue to the location of the future light metals plants. Norway, Holland and other maritime states could easily fill the gap left by the German shipyards—and not with submarines either.

While the exact location of new industries will depend upon all sorts of unpredictable factors, the change in the industrial map of Europe will be profound. The continent will be able to use its raw materials, labor, potential power and other industrial assets to best advantage. It can become much stronger and more prosperous without German heavy industry to shackle its progress.

Chapter IV

A FUTURE FOR GERMANY

GERMANY'S ROAD TO PEACE LEADS TO the farm. The men and women in the German labor force can best serve themselves and the world by cultivating the German soil. Such a program offers security to us as well as food for Germany and her neighbors.

A great deal of the discussion as to whether or not the German people could exist without heavy industry has been in the realm of abstract debate. It can be settled only through studying the facts about Germany's labor force, the farm land available and the potential production under principles of modern scientific land use.*

Such a study leads inescapably to the conclusion that Germany without heavy industry has the manpower and the acreage to feed her people. It will involve hardship and hard work for several years. Probably there will be considerable unemployment in the difficult transition period. That will be true whether Germany is allowed to rebuild heavy industry or not.

The main consideration, however, is not discomfort and toil for Germany but peace for the world. If it were true, as some people have asserted, that thirty million Germans would starve through the elimination of their heavy indus-

* Figures on German food production, consumption and imports will be found in Appendix A.

try, their misery could become a menace to peace. But a study of the facts shows that their best chance of getting an adequate diet within a reasonable time is by growing their own food and not by returning to steel mills and synthetic plants.

The last adequate German census was taken in 1933 and listed a population of 69,000,000. Agriculture accounted for 29 per cent of the labor force (all those at work or seeking work) or 9,388,000. In considering the question of whether Germany can feed herself from her own resources, the manpower part of the problem consists of getting enough workers formerly in industry onto the land.

The war has cost Germany millions of men at their most productive age. Cessions of certain parts of the prewar Germany can be taken for granted, and not all the population will be transferred to the smaller Reich, for not all of it was German. Therefore the best estimates of the postwar German population range between 55,000,000 and 60,000,000. Based on the latter figure, the labor force would not be far from 25,000,000.

Out of that number, it should be possible—within a reasonable time and with the sacrifices of comfort and leisure which the Germans formerly made for war—to place 5,000,000 more workers on the farms, bringing the total agricultural labor force up to 14,000,000.

That would leave 11,000,000 workers to be employed in Germany's transportation, trade, public services and light industries. It is worth noting that even under the pressure of war preparation in 1939, total employment in the group of heavy industries to be forbidden Germany was only a little over 4,000,000.

The exact methods by which the 5,000,000 new workers will be transferred to the farms is a German problem. But the way in which it might be done can be indicated.

If the German people are to make the best use of their soil, they are going to have to substitute the work of human hands for machinery for several years to come. The world's entire output of tractors, combines and so on will be needed by Germany's victims for a long time. Even with the increased plant facilities in this country and England, it will take years to supply the farms of ourselves and our Allies. The Germans will have to rely upon themselves. That means intensive cultivation of the best food crops possible.

More production of high nutrition crops can be obtained on small farms, especially when the big machines that make large-scale agriculture profitable are missing. Germany will have to break up the big estates to settle her extra 5,000,000 farm workers productively on family farms. At two workers to the family, this would mean 2,500,000 new farms.

Americans have made an experiment in recent years which proves how families can be settled on the land and made self-supporting while contributing to the nation's food supply. The Farm Security Administration has provided the kind of help Germany will need to give her new farmers. It consists of credit, advice, seed and tools. In the same way, Germany will have to give her 2,500,000 families displaced from other occupations the credit to take up land.

These families will have to get seed, fertilizer, tools, the materials to build a house. They will have to struggle hard, working long hours with little return at first. Perhaps many of them will have to fell trees to build their homes, then clear the wooded land to plant their crops—a tough job in any country.

But it is far better that they be so employed—both for them and us—than that they engage in the equally arduous task of rebuilding the Krupp Works at Essen.

In our own experience, we know that concentrated effort can settle 2,500,000 families in this way without much delay. In this country, we hardly scratched the surface of the possible advantages because we did not need them as badly as Germany does now. Yet in the year of our most critical food needs, it was this type of farmer who contributed the greatest proportional increase to our supplies.

In 1942, the year the war looked blackest for us, the Farm Security Administration was giving aid to 464,000 farm families. This was about 7 per cent of all the farm families in the country, but that 7 per cent accounted among other things for:

38 per cent of our increased milk production
11 per cent of our increased beef production
17 per cent of our increased dry bean crop
11 per cent of our increased peanut production

All of these are highly nutritive items, especially important in war or in the type of food emergency that faces Germany today. Many of our farmers have set records like these with even poorer soil than Germany's new farmers will have to use.

Henry Clark is typical of many thousands in this country. A dozen years ago he was a worker in Knoxville, Tennessee. By 1933, workers like Henry Clark had been through some very bad times, and in 1934 this one decided the land offered a better living than industry.

Henry took his family out into the Tennessee mountains and bought fifty-five acres of badly eroded, desolate hillside full of gullies and weeds. Folks round about shook their heads. The last man who farmed that piece of land, they told Henry, used to plant his corn by standing on a neighboring hill and shooting the seed into his own steep slopes with a shotgun.

Henry grinned and went to work. His first year he got a mighty scant crop of hay and corn—about two hundred dollars worth all told. But he stuck at it. He contour-plowed the slopes to prevent erosion, spread lime and phosphate liberally with the aid of the Soil Conservation Service, slowly brought the land back to life. In his tenth year on the farm, Henry Clark sold $4,600 worth of hay, tomatoes, dairy products, poultry and tobacco.

The German worker from Dortmund or Breslau won't have fifty-five acres. But he won't have steep slopes and completely exhausted soil either. The success of Henry Clark could be repeated in a smaller way and with variations by millions of Germans.

German industry, in the decades that Germany has been a menace to the peace of the world, occupied so large a place in the eyes of most observers that they quite failed to see behind it to the solid strength of German agriculture. Nor did they discover that the potential strength is greater even than the actual. In all Europe before the war, only France and Russia had more arable land than Germany. She is fortunate in the amount of arable land per person, too. France and Denmark have a little more in proportion to population, but Belgium and the Netherlands, which are among the richest agricultural states in the world, have far less. Germany is luckier than most of her neighbors in the proportion of her total area now suitable for crops. Already her arable land is 40.8 per cent of the whole country. France has only 37.5 per cent and Belgium 35.4 per cent, although Denmark has 62 per cent.

On the average, German acres before the war did not produce as much as those of some neighboring countries. The accompanying chart shows how in yield per acre Germany was outdistanced by others in the very crops which were the foundation of the Reich's agriculture.

GERMANY CAN CULTIVATE MORE EFFICIENTLY

Production on Pre-War European Farms in Quintals per Hectare

WHEAT		RYE		SUGAR BEETS	
Denmark	35	Belgium	25	Denmark	374
Netherl'ds	34	Netherl'ds	23	Sweden	361
Belgium	32	Sweden	20	Netherl'ds	349
Germany	27	Germany	20	Germany	304

BARLEY		OATS		POTATOES	
Denmark	34	Denmark	31	Netherl'ds	250
Netherl'ds	33	Netherl'ds	30	Belgium	221
Belgium	29	Belgium	29	Denmark	181
Germany	25	Germany	24	Germany	176

The following table shows at a glance that the land use could be greatly improved by a program of intensive cultivation. The total area of prewar Germany, before her grabs at Austria, Czechoslovakia, etc., was 116,000,000 acres. It was used thus:

Use	*Acres*	*Per Cent of Total*
Crop lands and orchards	47,100,000	40.6
Meadows and pastures	23,100,000	20.0
Forest and woodlands	32,200,000	27.7
Unproductive and wastelands	4,200,000	3.6
Buildings, roads, recreation grounds, military camps, etc.	9,400,000	8.1
	116,000,000	100.0

On those farm lands, incompletely as they were used, the Germans just before the war were raising 83 per cent of all the food they consumed, and the average German's diet was one of the richest in the world—only 6 per cent less than that of the average American. It is half again as much as the minimum standard that the Allies are trying to give the liberated people of Europe, the victims of German aggression, during the transition period until their own economies are functioning again.

In addition to that, the Germans raised another 5½ per cent of their prewar diet by feeding imported fodder to their own animals. About 11½ per cent was imported food for human consumption.

It seems plain, therefore, that without becoming even as good farmers as the Danes, Germans within a few years could be raising on their own soil at least 95 per cent of their real needs. They could also have enough farm exports to pay for fertilizer and the other 5 per cent of their food which cannot be raised in Germany. They would accomplish these other highly desirable results:

1. Give employment to several million workers displaced from industry.
2. Break the economic power of the Junkers, who have been the most persistent warmongers in Europe for generations.
3. Build up the small farmer as the backbone of a peaceful, perhaps a democratic nation.
4. (And this one would make the program worth while even without the other three.) Permit the rest of Europe to go about its business of building peace without the ever-present, haunting fear of German aggression.

These conclusions stem irresistibly from a study of German agriculture as it is and as it might easily become. The facts are unaccountably overlooked by those who take for granted that by some law of nature Germany is a country dependent upon industry for its living.

One of the facts which it seems very odd that anyone can overlook is the existence of Germany's 107,000,000 acres of land in farms and woods. About two-thirds of the total area was crop land and pasture. Germany's crop land alone is bigger than the total area of England and Wales; her acreage in farms is about double the size of all Great Britain. That is quite a sizable piece of land to escape notice.

Not all of Germany's 107,000,000 acres of farms will remain within the Reich after final boundary adjustments have been made. But it is better to leave her land than factories. Therefore, the plan set forth in these pages is based on the cession to other nations of East Prussia, Silesia, the Saar, some territory west of the Rhine, Schleswig-Holstein and a few much smaller areas. It also takes into account the internationalization of the Ruhr, and the eventual return of its German population to the Reich. All of these territories add up to a little more than 20,000,000 acres.

This would very closely balance the loss in population. The districts lost, as indicated here, amount to 18 per cent of Germany's total land area. Placing her postwar population at 60,000,000, the loss in human beings would be 15 per cent. The amount of arable land per person would remain about the same, and on the average the farms left in Germany would be as good as those taken from her.

If Germany makes a serious attempt to feed herself, she can do so. The use of low-cost labor will make up for the loss of territory and machinery. But we can expect her to make the effort only if she is forced to it by refusal of the United Nations to take over the responsibility from the German people. If we feed them ourselves—and it would have to be from stores of food which hungry millions of our allies need—the Germans will not undertake the necessary agricultural reform. They will, if they run true to their form of the last one hundred years, prefer to intrigue for a return of heavy industry and war.

It appears to be well within the limits of probability that if Germany makes full use of her land, she can do more than feed herself. Eventually she will be able to export produce to her neighbors and grow raw materials for the products of her light industries.

The great source of land for the future small farmers of

Germany lies in the great estates which not only retarded the course of German land reform but bred the race of Junkers who have been the backbone of the German General Staff, the most ardent warmongers in Europe and the core of German aggression.

In 1938, fewer than 7,000 Junker families owned almost one-fourth of all German land in farms. They and their satellite landowners of large estates, 34,000 in all, owned more than one-third of the land. The other 3,200,000 farm families owned less than two-thirds.

Their enormous estates gave the Junkers the political power which did so much to keep alive the harsh militarism of Germany. That somewhat obscured the fact that they were as omnipotent and as harsh in German agriculture.

The political and military careers of the Junkers as well as the ostentation of their society were financed by a worse than feudal exploitation of an impoverished farm labor class. The wages and working conditions of Germans were held down by importing foreign laborers. The use of prisoners as slaves on these estates during the war was no more than a slight variation on a long-established policy.

Most of the Junkers were as backward in their farming as in their social outlook. Rather primitive agricultural techniques prevailed. Large areas were kept as hunting preserve. Much of the rest was used for crude grains instead of making the most of the land from higher grade food crops and cattle.

In breaking up the big estates, Allied interests coincide

perfectly with German welfare. Many Germans know that they have suffered in the past because Junker influence set the Reich's agrarian policy from the days of Bismarck. And that policy has been one of high protection for Junker crops.

The high tariff on fodder ruined peasants who were dependent upon it to feed their animals. Thousands of formerly independent farmers were thrown upon the non-existent mercy of the Junkers. Even under the republic, with Chancellor Bruening in nominal power, the duty on barley was more than doubled.

The result of high tariffs was as bad for the German consumer as for the German peasant. In 1931, the price of a kilo (2.2 pounds) of wheat bread in Belgium was 20 pfennigs; in Germany more than 80 pfennigs. In 1935 wheat sold at 69.50 marks a ton in Rotterdam and more than 200 marks in Germany. That same year the German price of sugar was ten times what it was in the world market.

Protective tariffs of this kind placed a strait-jacket on the development of agriculture in Germany. The most inefficient form of production was protected, the extensive cereal growing of the larger Junker estates. Elimination of the Junker protective economy will free millions of German farmers from bonds that have restricted their markets. They will not only be able to feed their own countrymen, but they will be able to contribute to the enormous task of banishing from Europe the specter of hunger, which the German war machine evoked.

It seems plain that land reform has long been overdue

in Germany for purely agricultural reasons quite as much as for security and ethical ones. Alexander Gerschendron, an agrarian expert who has made a careful study of the problem in *Bread and Democracy*, thinks the Junker economy and political power defeated democratic beginnings in Germany after 1918. He says:

> German democracy rejected the road of agrarian revolution, the road traveled by most of the countries in which the economic power of large estate owners was curbed after the World War. . . . Translated into the realistic language of practical politics, this meant that the Junkers had been rescued again. . . .
>
> Politically, the position of the Junkers improved steadily. The big estates quickly became the rallying places for young men—flotsam of the war—who found it difficult to return to the normal life of peace. Little armies of vigilantes were organized and rearmed at the Junker estates. They were kept in preparedness for an attack upon the Republic.

Ever since Bismarck's time, encouragement of more small farms has been a dream of a good many Germans. Bismarck himself introduced a plan for homesteads which the Junkers always were able to nullify. The demand for land reform was a continuing political institution and every new agitator seeking popularity played upon it. As just one example, the greatest agitator of them all, Hitler, proclaimed as one of his twenty-five points in 1921: "We demand agrarian reform consistent with our national needs; the passage of a law to expropriate without compensation land which is to be used for common purposes. . . ."

He changed it later, but it is indicative of German

desires that he felt it necessary to pay lip service to the very human yearning to get "back to the land."

The 34,000 big landowners of Germany, and particularly the Junkers, have shown themselves unworthy cultivators of their 37,000,000 acres, as well as a collective peril to the peace of mankind. They had only 12,725,000 acres in crops. Their land, suitably divided, would enable hundreds of thousands of peasants who own less than five acres apiece to have enough to utilize their full labor productively.

Or if 24,000,000 acres were divided up into twelve-acre farms, 2,000,000 families totaling several million individuals could be settled on new homesteads. Twelve acres are more than the average prewar German peasant owned. Still more workers could make farms out of reclaimed wasteland, military camps, airfields and so on. The rest of the new agricultural workers would have to clear forest for their farms or bring pasture under the plow.

Millions of man-years of good hard work could be put into draining swamps, terracing hills for cultivation, clearing cut-over forest, putting back into productive use the vast acreage ruined by being turned into army camps, artillery proving grounds, training fields, etc.

The transition from factory to farm will be much easier for Germans than for most urban dwellers. Even more than with us, the present generation of industrial workers has been recruited from farms. An even greater number are the sons and daughters of farmers. Besides, the German worker has kept a closer touch with the soil than most others. Millions of them have had subsistence gardens which were often almost small farms of anything up to an acre. Even before the Nazis came to power Berlin alone counted 198,000 such garden plots within the city limits and 247,000 in surrounding territory; Hamburg had 96,000 inside the city.

The Nazis intensified this practice, and in addition sent all youths out for a few weeks each year to work on real farms. The combinations of these factors makes millions of German workers almost farmers before they get their land.

The simplest answer to the argument that Germany cannot feed herself without heavy industry, is the fact that in the past she was very nearly self-sufficient in food, partly through the increased production drive in anticipation of war.

The average German table groaned with a variety and quantity of food that would make the mouths of her neighbors water, and most of it was grown at home. Bread, potatoes, sugar, fats and oils, meat, poultry and milk accounted for 90 per cent of German nourishment in the years 1933-1937. All the potatoes, sugar and milk were raised within the Reich. She imported 2 per cent of her breadstuffs and 3 per cent of the meat and poultry. A very little more intensive agriculture, even in her reduced area would eliminate the necessity for these imports. Of fats and oils, 53 per cent were imported, and the imported share accounted for 8 per cent of the total German diet.

The postwar Reich will have to import some food after it is rebuilt for peace, but with the improvement of small farms and the consequent production of more hogs, the imports could be greatly reduced. The other principal prewar imports, all negligible in total, were fresh vegetables, cheese, dry legumes, eggs—all of which could be raised at home—fruits, nuts, fish, cocoa and coffee.

In total weight, this average German diet totted up to 1.3 pounds per person per day, and amounted to 3,030 calories. The average daily consumption in the United States is 3,200 calories.

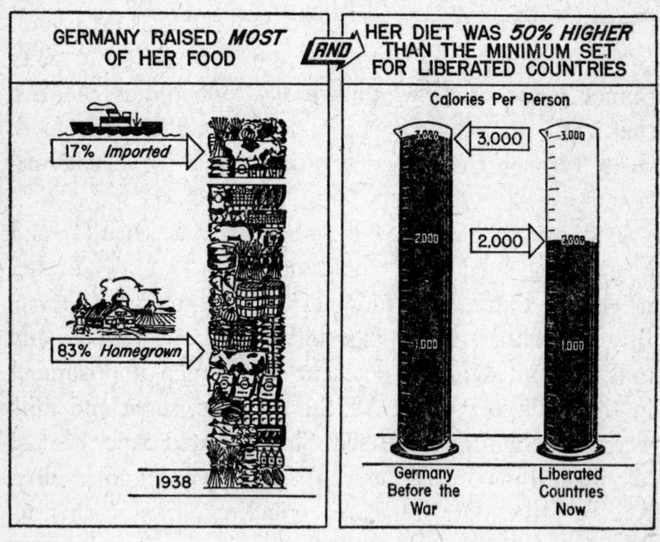

The application of 55 per cent more labor to German farms, as proposed here, will not increase this food supply by 55 per cent. But that will not be necessary. An extra 15 per cent would make Germany virtually self-sustaining, even on her high prewar diet. But more probably, Germans will eat a little less for they will have to export food as well as consumer goods in return for such products of heavy industry as they will need, the small amount of foodstuffs that will not grow in Germany and the rather large amount of nitrates and phosphates she will require to keep her soil productive.

Intensive farm cultivation offers Germany a solution to her employment problem as well as to her food problem. With millions of her industrial workers unemployed while the machinery of total war is dismantled and replaced by an economy of peace, Germany faces as difficult a reconversion task as any nation of the world. These millions of unemployed can be put to work much more quickly on the land than by waiting for factories to be rebuilt and re-equipped.

Even if the safety of Europe did not demand that most of them become farmers, the immediate needs of their own country would. Germans will have to raise their own food within a few years no matter what course the United Nations take, short of starving Allies for the sake of enemies. There will be little enough for a long time for the Belgians, Hollanders, Poles, Greeks, Czechs, Yugoslavs and others who have been hungry for years because the Germans plunged the world into war.

Furthermore, the twelve-acre farms of former steel, chemical and electrical workers can get into production a great deal more rapidly than the steel mills of Essen. Under current world conditions, the only way we can be sure sixty million Germans will eat is to get a great many of them on the land as soon as possible, and keep them there.

Chapter V

INDUSTRIAL COUNTER REVOLUTION

GERMANY MAINTAINED HER ascendancy over the industries of the rest of Europe only by an extremely unnatural overemphasis on employment in factories. Moreover, the workers were not engaged in turning out goods to raise the standard of living of the German people and their neighbors. Years before the first overt blow was struck, German industry was geared for war. An industrial counterrevolution is obviously needed to correct this lopsided economy.

The initial steps toward getting the wheels of German production started for peace have not indicated too great an awareness of that need. Hardly were the zones of occupation formally set than we began to hear that since Allied troops were on German soil, German factories would be used to supply them. The result foreseen at that time was unemployment among our friends who are Germany's neighbors while our armies gave jobs to Germans. Then on July 20, Drew Middleton wrote to the New York *Times* from Frankfurt:

> During the last ten days this correspondent has found that increased emphasis is being placed by military government officials on the maintenance of industry. This is explained by what was described to me by one source as an "urgent need" for materiel in the Pacific. One wonders whether need is urgent enough to warrant the

> maintenance of a part of the industry of one enemy nation to defeat another.
>
> The Bosch factory may work for the United States today producing equipment for the war in the East. If the plant is maintained, who will it work for tomorrow? . . . The question that inevitably will arise is whether the United States can sanction the reopening of a tractor factory to make agricultural machinery, knowing that when control has been removed the plant can be converted into a tank factory.

The same dangerous philosophy that worried Mr. Middleton was in evidence among the men who had to grapple with Europe's almost frighteningly difficult coal problem. Weakened by very slim food rations, the people of the war-torn Continent are facing a winter tragically short of fuel. Months after the Allies entered the Ruhr, the mines there were operating at about 3 per cent of capacity. Yet Allied studies showed that between June 1945, and April, 1946, a minimum of 25,000,000 tons would have to be shipped from the Ruhr to other parts of Europe, not including Germany. The same studies indicated that the mines, machinery and transportation were not too badly damaged to achieve this objective. The shortage was in men able and willing to work.

Obviously Germans should be mining that coal for Europe until they can be replaced by workers from outside. Allied experts found that lack of food prevented men from doing a day's work at the coal face, but army food was urged to correct that. The other big reason for lack of manpower was absenteeism, and the experts proposed to cure that by turning the management of the mines back to their old masters! A worse device, whether from the standpoint of immediate production or the achievement of our avowed war aims, could hardly be imagined. The management of the mines has been thoroughly Nazified. Among the bosses are men who can remember how successfully the sabotage of production in the Ruhr defeated Allied reparation collection twenty years ago. And Allied councils are not lacking in men who declare that the real reason for such a small coal production in the Ruhr is German sabotage today. Yet the theory that Germans know best about Ruhr coal prevailed, and among the officials recommended for a top management job in over-all Ruhr coal production was Hugo Stinnes, son of the Ruhr magnate who did more than any other single industrialist to bring Hitler to power.

The rebuilding of German factories, the uses of the Stinneses to achieve Allied objectives are a long way from the path to peace which most Americans want to follow. It may serve to get us back on the right road if we examine the kind of industry Germany had in the past and just what it would be safe to leave her in the future. The 1933 German census showed that her men and women working or seeking work were distributed as follows:

Occupation	*Workers*	*Per Cent of Labor Force*
Agriculture	9,388,000	29
Industry	13,235,000	41
Trade, commerce and transportation	5,994,000	18
Public service and services	2,725,000	8
Domestic service	1,280,000	4
	32,622,000	100

That is very topheavy on industry, even for a highly industrialized country. By way of comparison the United States census of 1940, which uses a somewhat different classification, showed that the 45,500,000 Americans gainfully employed in April in the greatest industrial country in the world, were divided:

		Per Cent of Labor
Agriculture	9,000,000	20
Industry	12,500,000	27
Trade, finance and services	11,000,000	24
Transportation and utilities	3,000,000	6½
Public service	4,000,000	9½
Self-employed, domestics, etc.	6,000,000	13
	45,500,000	100

At that time 7,800,000 were unemployed. Even if half of them were industrial workers, the United States percentage of the labor force classed as industrial workers would be only about 30 per cent as against Germany's 41 per cent.

It is true, of course, that the output per man was much higher in the United States. But the figures also answer those who argue that Germans have a natural genius for industry and can work at it better than other Europeans. The topheavy German industrial structure was maintained only by this artificial concentration of workers in mines and factories.*

Before the industrial revolution, which came to Germany a full century after it had transformed England and without any gradual German transition from feudalism at all, about 80 per cent of the population of the Reich was

* Figures on prewar German industrial employment will be found in Appendix B.

engaged in agriculture. There probably were about ten million workers on the land—roughly the same number as in 1939. The abolition of German heavy industry would not make the country 80 per cent agricultural again, but it would free the workers needed to achieve virtual self-sufficiency in food. Four million of them would come

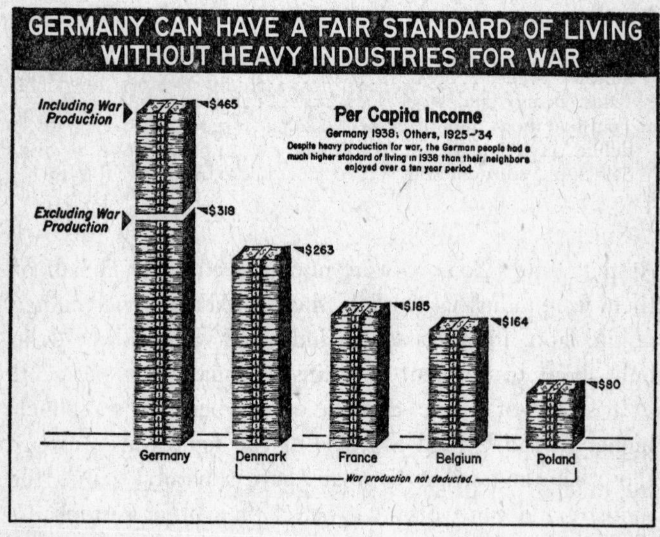

from the eliminated industries on the basis of 1939 employment in those industries.

But Germany would retain a substantial and busy manufacturing life after the period of transition. Probably almost seven million workers would be engaged in manufacturing, mining and construction, which is about the same proportion that were employed in these fields in peacetime United States. But instead of the enormous number of service industries in this country, Germany would have farms. In some ways, the service industries are an index of a nation's standard of living. A lot of them mean comforts and luxuries quite widely spread. Few of them mean a more Spartan life for the average citizen.

If peace is to be secure, Germans will be deprived of the luxuries of life for quite a long time. They will have fewer writers, lawyers, teachers and engineers. There will be a very big decrease in the number of waiters, taxicab drivers, barbers and clerks. Maybe the personal servant, beautician, clothing model and fashionable furrier will virtually disappear. Certainly the Germans will see a marked decline in places of entertainment, florists, cafés and retail shops of all kinds.

Furthermore, whatever else may happen, the German people in the immediate future can count upon a period of mass unemployment as severe as anything they have ever known. The destruction of many factories during the war will prevent the employment of millions. The long concentration on war, which for many years claimed two-thirds of all Germany's national production, will make the task of reconversion to peace even more difficult and protracted than with us, throwing still more Germans out of work.

Even for factories which remain standing and can produce for peace without much reconversion, such as food processing plants, textile mills and so on, there is the question of getting raw materials and replacements or new parts for machinery long neglected because of the devotion of all energies and equipment to munitions. The task will be a long one even if the United Nations place German desires for these items ahead of French,

Czech or Dutch needs. Germany has no foreign exchange to buy. Even with help which cannot be given unless we are willing to connive at gross injustice to the victims of the German war machine, the Reich can only put men back to work slowly in any industry.

Adding all these factors together, it seems unlikely that Germany could achieve within the next few years a level of nonagricultural employment as high as she had in 1933. The depression will be at least as bad. Based on the number of Germans employed in 1939, that would mean a postwar unemployment for Germans of 10,000,000, which would also seem to be a minimum for some time to come unless many go on the land. The manufacturing, mining and construction industries alone would drop 7,800,000 from the payrolls, even if heavy industry were to be left on the 1933 basis. (That was the year the Nazis really started the war.) Another 2,200,000 would be jobless in the service trades, transportation, public service and public utilities.

The existence of millions of destitute and probably desperate families would be an offense both to humanity and to world security. The only practical solution is to put most of them to work on the land and in labor battalions outside Germany repairing the damage they have done. But once the postwar chaos has been reduced to some kind of order, most of the industries which Germany could normally acquire will be able to revive. On the basis of 1933 statistics—and with the elimination of heavy industry—that would give an industrial population of 6,660,000 divided approximately as follows:

Mines and quarries	900,000
Optical products (nonmilitary)	100,000
Textiles	850,000
Paper and allied products	190,000
Printing and allied industries	275,000
Leather and leather products	120,000
Rubber products (not synthetics)	50,000
Sawmills, furniture and wooden goods	610,000
Musical instruments	40,000
Food processing, etc.	1,450,000
Apparel and other fabricated textiles	1,050,000
Construction	1,025,000

This list gives pretty much the measure of the industries Germany should be allowed to retain. With 5,000,000 or 6,000,000 in transportation, public utilities and trade, they offer her a well rounded life for her people. Of course it will take years. But she will be able to achieve full employment without the opportunity for hasty conversion of industry to a war basis. Actually, in 1933 the employment in the forbidden industries was 1,797,602 for all of Germany which ought to remain within her borders. By 1939 war preparations had sent German heavy industry's employment up by 133 per cent. The rest of German industry employed 70 per cent more workers.

These remaining industries will give Germany what she needs to support her people and even to export in order to buy essentials she cannot produce herself—or essentials which she will not be allowed to produce such as machinery, transportation equipment and the like. Her share in world trade will be smaller than it used to be, but then it had been on the decline for a great many years. Before World War I, Germany accounted for 12 per cent of the world's international commerce. By the 1920's her share had fallen below 10 per cent. In 1936 and

1937 it was a bit more than 8 per cent. The world would not be the loser if Germany fell to 2 or 3 per cent and her share taken over by other nations.

A reduction in this trade will make it easier to control the German exports and imports to insure against clandestine armaments and research into new methods of death. Germany will have to import a certain amount of metal or metal products for such homely items as nails, hammers, screw drivers and spare parts of machinery. But imports of steel should be checked to see that amounts in excess of needs for needles, razors, etc., are not slipping through. An even closer check on chemicals and the apparatus for scientific research must be made.

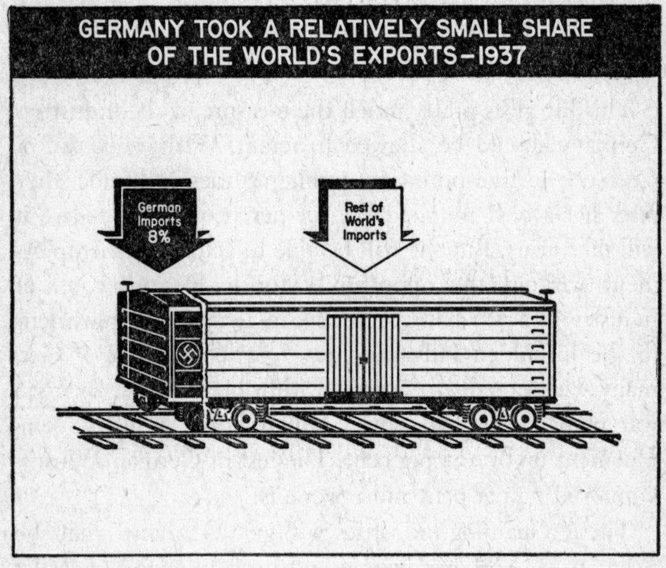

Even if the memorandum of the meeting in Strasbourg's Rotes Haus had not proved the importance that the Nazis attach to scientific laboratories, the whole course of German preparations for aggression would give us the key to their methods. Germany has made a great many notable contributions to science, and especially in the warlike discoveries. It must be one of the aims of Allied policy to circumvent the plans of German leaders to organize hidden laboratories for war under the guise of studying the peaceful sciences, whether pure or applied.

The nature of modern research gives us the clue to our course. The solitary inventor working alone, in secret and in poverty is not the source of most of our industrial progress any longer. Research is organized on a large scale, with a great deal of method, a great deal of apparatus and a great many workers. The sum of their toil frequently adds up to genius, but it would not have given practical results if that many scientists had been working individually without co-ordination of effort.

Therefore, the teeth can be drawn from Germany's scientific war machine by forbidding the organization of the elaborate laboratories of her past. Elimination of heavy industry will help here, because it is precisely these industries which have sponsored the most research. The electrical, metallurgical and chemical industries generally account for most of the factory-financed research in any large country.

Equal vigilance must be directed to rooting out centers of German research abroad. Those centers already have been established; they were part of the careful German preparation for defeat, since the Germans, as we now know, began preparing for World War III just after they passed their high tide of conquest in World War II. On the basis of evidence now available, this preparation to carry on scientific studies under foreign cloaks began in 1943. Consider this extract from the testimony of Assistant Secretary of State W. L. Clayton before the Kilgore Committee on June 25, 1945:

> In a certain neutral country, the German electrical company, Telefunken, bought a plant in the summer of 1943. The plant was immediately modernized and enlarged. It now has complete facilities for testing the most intricate short wave radio equipment, and magnificently equipped laboratories for research in the ultra short wave and tone frequency field. As late as April of this year negotiations were in progress for the importation of skilled German technicians to work in this plant.
>
> In another neutral country . . . a semi-official German organization presented a proposal to the government . . . for the equipment and establishment of a technical school system . . . The acceptance of this offer by the neutral government would have necessitated the employment of a large number of German teachers and technicians. . . .
>
> Aircraft repair establishments in the same neutral country ordered certain specialized machines from German suppliers in 1941. They were unable to obtain delivery until late in 1943, at which time they received, not the amount of equipment that they ordered, but five times as much. Much of this machinery, adaptable to the large scale manufacture of aircraft, rests today in this neutral country, still uncrated.

It will not be possible to prevent German scientists from setting up laboratories in their homes or hidden in barns. But it will be possible to check the importation of scientific equipment, without which their work will be extremely slow if not impossible. It will be possible to deprive them of their organized centers of research, which will make it difficult for them to gain the benefit of each other's experiments.

There will remain to Germany her medical laboratories and the like. They will not be a substitute for the research once carried out in the Reich. The result may well be that the world will have to wait for a few discoveries of benefit to its health and well-being until they are made by non-Germans. The experience of the past is that the sum of all the lives saved by German discoveries would represent but a tiny fraction of the lives expended in fighting the two world wars, to which German scientific genius contributed much more than it did to the arts of peace.

Chapter VI

REPARATIONS

BY THE TIME FRANCE HAD FINISHED paying off Germany after the Franco-Prussian War, French industry and trade had grown so strong that Bismarck is said to have remarked ruefully that the next time he beat the French he would insist Germany pay the indemnity. The exaggeration serves to emphasize the dangers concealed behind the alluring façade of reparations.

The basis of the apocryphal Bismarck story is that payment of the 1871 indemnity did not in the least weaken France. The total required was the then astronomical sum of one billion dollars. France paid it off in cash by 1873. She seemed all the healthier, economically speaking, for having made the effort.

Cash indemnities no longer have any place in practical negotiations. The substitution of reparations in kind avoids the difficulties of transfer. It also tends to keep the amounts smaller, since statesmen are more realistic about goods than about money. But reparations in kind do not avert the basic danger. Unless the items to be taken by the Allies are carefully selected, the payment of reparations, especially over any protracted period, will build up German industry.

So far as reparations were paid by Germany after World War I, that is what happened. She was obliged to build up her industries and her exports to meet even the relatively small payments she made.

In the 1920's, German reparations caused a good deal of dissension in Allied ranks. Each nation was dissatisfied with what it got and believed others were faring better. The French, for example, were sometimes a little jealous as they contrasted the meager flow of goods and cash which came their way with the confiscated merchant ships which fell to England's lot. Englishmen, who found the ships slower and more expensive to operate than the fine new ones Germany was building for herself, were inclined to think France got a better bargain in German coal. This feeling was all the stronger when Britain's sales of coal to France fell off because of German deliveries. Meanwhile, Germany blossomed out with a brand new merchant marine built in yards which would be turning out submarines a few years later. In order to make delivery of industrial goods to France and others, Germany was allowed to convert arms plants to civilian uses and keep them going—with exceedingly slim returns to France in the way of reparations—until she was ready to convert them back to war.

Besides retaining all the bad features of the Franco-Prussian settlement, the Allies after 1919 added a worse one of their own devising. France in the seventies paid in full two years and four months after peace was signed. The Allies in the twenties tried to keep Germany paying, first for forty-two years, then for more than sixty. These terms were favored by some Allied spokesmen, who wished to weaken Germany, because they thought the Reich would be kept bowed down under the burden through two generations. The terms were favored also by some advocates of leniency because they thought the long period would make it easier for Germany to pay.

Both overlooked a fundamental economic fact. No such long-term payments are possible without the co-operation of the debtor. A creditor can seize what the debtor already has, but he has to have the debtor's help to get the produce of the debtor's later toil. The Allies were in the position of a bank that holds a $10,000 mortgage on a farm which would not bring $2,000 at a foreclosure sale. The only way the bank can get its money back is to enlist the farmer's co-operation in improving his land and crops to increase his income. If the bank has no confidence in the farmer, it would do well to write off the loss and hope it won't happen again.

The Allies did not want to follow either course. So they found themselves seeking to persuade Germany to produce for reparations by concessions which were virtually bribes. One of the first was permission to convert war plants which might otherwise have been destroyed. That was a real bargain for Germany. Then Germany argued for foreign loans, and used at least part of them to build up her industries, ostensibly for reparations but actually for war. And finally, she bargained for evacuation of the Rhineland. This was when she agreed to accept the Young plan of 1929. The Allies marched out of the Rhineland in 1930. The last German reparations payment was made in 1931. The Allies were poorer by the amount they had lent to Germany; it was more than the reparations paid and they never collected on the loans. Germany was richer by the cash and, more important, by the greatly increased industrial plant.

Reparations were a running sore in the whole world economy of the twenties, but there was one short period when deliveries were made without adding anything to Germany's strength and without costing the Allies trade or jobs of their own. This was in the first couple of years after the war when Germany paid out of her assets abroad and her supplies at home. By May 1, 1921, Germany herself figured these payments at more than five billion dollars. The Allies put them at about two billion dollars. Whatever the figure, it represented reparations which helped the Allies and added nothing to Germany.

The point is of practical importance today. Reparations in the form of goods already made by Germans can give immense impetus to reconstruction in all the devastated lands of Europe. Such goods might be a substantial portion of the physical assets now existing in Germany. They would consist of the loot seized by the Nazis in every country they conquered. They would include also German machinery of all kinds, stocks of raw materials, gasoline, livestock, railroad equipment, barges, fabricated steel—in short, a whole catalogue of useful manufactures for Allied consumers and industries. German labor, to operate the equipment or to work on the farms and in rebuilding ruined areas, may be needed for years by the liberated countries. They should get it.

Obviously, however, all of Germany's assets will hardly make much of a dent in the gigantic job of reconstruction. And just as obviously, ordinary justice demands that the Germans pay for the damage they have done, no matter how long it takes. But there are several catches in that simple proposition. One is that the Germans have destroyed more than they could possibly replace. Another is that the acceptance of German-made reparations in great volume and over a long period will weaken the very countries most in need of strengthening. Finally, and most serious of all, the payment of such reparations will build up German industry to its old dangerously dominant place in the European economy. We know from experience how the thing would work.

First of all, the United Nations themselves would have to help rebuild German industry so the schedule of reparations could be met. Germany ended World War I with her factories intact, for there had been no fighting on her soil and no mass bombing of her cities. This time her whole system of production and transportation has been bombed and shelled. Furthermore, it was far more thoroughly converted to war work than in 1914-1918, so the process of reconversion, except in those basic industries which are the same in war or peace, would be more complicated. Instead of taking German equipment to help her victims, we would have to supply Germany with still more equipment, probably American. But anything we can send to Germany will have to be taken away from what we could send to the liberated areas. We would be rebuilding a German factory rather than a French or Dutch or Russian plant. It is hard enough to apportion the available equipment among our friends without giving priority to our enemies.

Yet Germany cannot pay recurring reparations unless we do just that. She has no great raw material resources upon which to draw, except coal—and that ought to be taken from her anyway through international control of the Ruhr.

This does not exhaust the objections to reparations which take the form of industrial products. The devastated countries of Europe which receive them would not be able or would not have so much incentive to build their own industries. They would be receiving German steel, German railway cars, German machines, German trucks and buses, German electrical goods, German textiles, German chemicals. They would become so dependent upon German industry that they would never be able to break away, and would find themselves helplessly caught in the German net as soon as the newly powerful Reich felt strong enough for another fling at war.

The dependence would continue long after reparations ended. All over Europe, the people would be equipped with and accustomed to German products. When a new part for a tractor or a dynamo was needed, it would have to be ordered from Germany to fit the existing machine. When new equipment was bought, it would be German because engineers and workers would have become used to it. Consumers would buy goods made in Germany because the packages would bear familiar brand names.

For the smaller countries, this means political as well as economic dependence upon Germany. By the same token, industrialization of these countries will make them more independent of any outside pressure, raise their standards of living and fit them to take a strong, free place in the community of nations. They know this well enough, and are eager to acquire new industries while rebuilding old ones. They know the opportunity is now, in the months and years just after the war. They know that one locomotive or one electric generator this year is worth ten in 1950. If the one goes to Germany, they will be justifiably bitter. They will have been saved in war only to be betrayed in peace.

Larger countries will suffer as much, and the United States will not be the least among them. For German reparations will sweep a market to which the trading nations of the world look for a necessary part of their postwar prosperity. Advocates of a heavy German schedule of recurring reparations are asking us to build up German industry at the direct expense of our own.

Consider steel as an example. The United States, Britain and Germany have all increased their production for war. Our own capacity is 90,000,000 tons a year. In 1937, one of the best of prewar years, we produced 57,000,000 tons and provided 40 per cent of the world's steel exports. Germany produced that year 22,000,000 tons; the United Kingdom, 15,000,000; France, 9,000,000. Out of the increased British and American capacity, not to mention the easily expanded French capacity, all postwar exports could easily be met. It would be good business to meet them. But if Germany is to retain her steel industry to pay reparations, Yugoslavia, Greece, Norway, the Netherlands and even France herself will be getting their steel from the Reich. The result: unemployment in Pittsburgh and Birmingham.

Industrial reparations would tend to tie the chemical industries of the world once more to a German-dominated cartel. Before the war, the leadership of the German trust imposed strict limitations on production. The United States has since then expanded its output about four times. Before the war, little was exported because of the German-imposed restrictions. With reasonable competitive opportunities in peacetime, the industry will be able

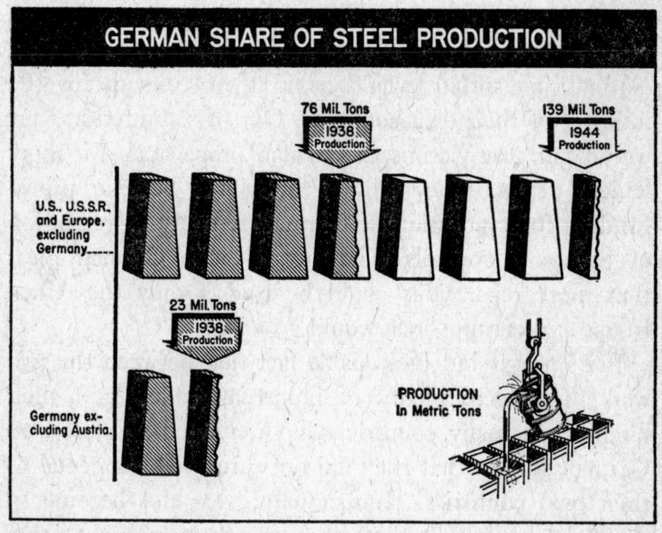

to sell in Europe. But not if Europe gets its chemicals by way of reparations from Germany.

The exporting nations among the Allies will be the first to agitate for cancellation of such recurring reparations. The competition from that source was one reason England was eager to reduce German payments in the twenties. It was responsible for a good deal of the American dislike of the program. But it is better never to impose such reparations at all than to end them as a result of a quarrel among the United Nations.

The quarrel would develop inevitably because receipt of reparations would create certain vested interests which would resent any stoppage. Even more dangerous to peace and Allied unity would be the fact that these vested interests would become pro-German interests, too. They would have a stake in the reconstruction of German industry far beyond any concern for that in other United Nations and often even beyond their concern for the industry of their own countries. Out of self-interest, they would fall easy victims to German propaganda for more lenient terms. They would themselves become propagandists for evacuation of German territory or relaxation of economic controls. They would echo German pleas that more reparations could be paid if only the Allied troops and commissions would go home.

It is an ugly but inescapable fact that between the two wars there were plenty of industrial leaders and their satellites in many countries who were tied so closely to German success that they did not care what happened to their own countries. Human nature has not become so purified by war that these men or others with the same characteristics will cease to exist. At best they would rouse dissension in their own countries. At worst they would contribute to the weakening of European industry in general and to encouraging German preparations for another war.

Such results indicate, too, the menace to the international economic measures which the United Nations hope to adopt for the restoration of world trade. The most important of these steps are removal of barriers to trade and stabilization of currencies as the medium through which that trade is carried on. We have hoped to eliminate quotas by which one country limits its imports of another's products to a certain percentage of previous sales or of the country's requirements. For example, before the Hawley-Smoot tariff (highest in our history), American radio sets were so much better than any others that 56 per cent of all French receivers were made in this country. In retaliation for the tariff, France slapped a quota on American sets, and set it at 8 per cent.

We have hoped to eliminate discriminatory tariffs and to set up international machinery to keep foreign exchanges stable. Reparations will upset all these applecarts. Countries receiving or even just hoping to receive German goods as reparations to sell to their citizens will be tempted to impose quotas on other nations. They will be tempted equally to raise tariffs. And they will tend to force controls over foreign exchange because their own exports will not be balanced by imports through normal trade channels. That, too, would be a fruitful source of United Nations discord.

It is often argued that a wholesome use of force would soon bring the Germans around to producing reparations. The limitations of force were discovered by the Nazis themselves in their attempts to squeeze occupied territory. Although they had men elaborately trained in brutality, they never were able to prevent sabotage and passive resistance. We would be equally helpless. Our people and our soldiers would grow weary eventually of wielding the lash over a stubborn though beaten population.

One of the best documented failures of force as a collection agent for reparations was experienced by the French and Belgians more than twenty years ago. For two and a half years, beginning on January 11, 1923, their troops were in the Ruhr Valley while their engineers grimly struggled to extract some sort of tangible benefits from the rich coal mines and the huge steel works. The Germans simply quit work, refused to run their factories or their railroads and left the valley in droves. The French jailed some of them and threatened many, but production could not be boosted with men in jail, and the example failed to bring workers back to their jobs. When the Dawes plan finally settled this particular dispute and the troops left the Ruhr on July 31, 1925, it was found that the total addition to the reparations payments had amounted to 798,000,000 gold marks. This was more than most other collection methods had extorted. But it was less than a third of Germany's minimum obligation under agreements she had accepted before the occupation.

The parallel to what has been happening in the Ruhr since the Allies entered the valley this year is perilously exact. The miners have been staying away from the pits, and the occupying authorities have been taking what is described as every possible measure to get them back. As we have seen, that means every possible measure short of cleaning out the old-line German management and endeavoring to revive some of the former German trade union movement to spur production. If the first attempts to extract coal for our freezing Allies were so futile when we had a newly victorious army in control and before any sort of organized German resistance had time to develop, the hopelessness of basing reparations collection on the same methods is obvious.

However, even if our force or our cunning were more successful in plucking a wealth of industrial products from Germany, the basic problem would not be affected. After all, the avowed object of any reparations program is to rebuild the devastated areas for whose ruin Germany is responsible. The best way to do that lies through three main routes, all of which would be locked rather than opened by a system of reparations paid in industrial products. The three may be summed up as:

1. *The largest possible immediate assistance to the liberated countries.* This means, besides whatever help can be given by the other United Nations, all the useful machinery, raw materials and labor that can be found in Germany. Reparations paid in industrial products over a long period of time would mean that we would have to divert these supplies now from the liberated countries to Germany and leave the Reich with her own industrial plant intact.

2. *Reconstruction and development of industries within the liberated countries.* This involves, among other things, the utmost extension of international trade possible. Recurring reparations provide only unfair competition for local industries and barriers to the free exchange of goods between nations.

3. *Security from aggression and the fear of aggression.* The first step here is to eliminate the German menace. If German heavy industries are destroyed, we have achieved the primary objective. Reparations in kind over a long period require more and even heavier German

industry, with an accompaniment of fear and insecurity throughout the United Nations.

The real test of the value of any reparations settlement is simple. Does it strengthen Germany's war-making potential? Then it is bad, no matter how profitable. Does it help our Allies without strengthening Germany? Then it is good.

Chapter VII

GERMANY AS AN ANTI RUSSIAN SMOKE SCREEN

ABOUT HALFWAY BETWEEN WORLD WAR I and World War II, commonly known as a period of peace but sometimes called more accurately "the long armistice," there was a strongly supported campaign to relieve Germany, along with other nations, of her debts to the United States for the year 1931-1932. And one of the main arguments for including Germany in such an arrangement ran like this:

"In her position in the center of Europe, Germany in good health would be a bulwark against instability and Communism."

That point of view was widely held by a variety of statesmen between the 1918 armistice and the outbreak of war in 1939. Nor can it be spoken of entirely in the past tense. Today it motivates a goodly proportion of those who expound the view that a strong Germany is an advantage to her recent enemies in the West.

The apologists for this thesis are even more dangerous to the cause of peace than their predecessors of the twenties and thirties. They are less frank. They do not openly say that we need Germany as a bulwark against Russia and Communism. For reasons which they undoubtedly regard as "statesmanlike" they prefer to operate behind smoke screens of more or less plausible explanations. They seem to feel that this is too delicate a question for the American people to discuss on its merits. They say they would not want to disturb the co-operation of Russia and the United States, ignoring the fact that evasion of the issue is far more disturbing than frank debate. As a result, the people could find themselves at odds with Russia over a point which this self-styled superior wisdom has not allowed them to understand, while at the same time Germany would have been permitted to recruit her strength for another era of aggression and war. The smoke screens behind which this desire to build up bulwarks against Russia is hidden are mainly these:

The utter fallacy that Europe needs a strong industrial Germany.

The shortsighted contention that recurring reparations (which would require immediate reconstruction of German industry) are necessary to make Germany pay for the destruction of which she is guilty.

The naïve belief that removal or demolition of all German war materials and arms plants would be enough to prevent Germany from waging another war.

The illogical assumption that kindness will stimulate the rise of a real German democracy committed to a peaceful policy.

The danger to America and the world is not to be found in these arguments so much as in the fact that some of those who put them forward press them without much real belief in their truth. If they avowed their actual motive, the people could be relied upon to repudiate the program promptly. Americans know that it is Germany they have had to fight twice in a quarter of a century, not Russia. They know that our soldiers were killed and our civilians torpedoed by Germans, not Russians. They know that our own industries have been hog-tied by German cartels, not Russian. They know that plans for the subjection of the Western Hemisphere were laid by Germans, not Russians.

It is a rather lame apology to say that these facts should not be aired in public because the Russians might learn how certain officials of the United States Government are thinking. Such disclosures, it is said, might endanger our relations with Russia at a critical moment. But the Russians are quite well aware of this attitude on the part of some of our own and our Allied officials. In daily dealings between governments, such a fundamental point of view soon makes itself evident.

It is a point of view to which we can trace many of the mistakes of "the long armistice." At the Paris peace conference in 1919, the assembled statesmen displayed an almost hysterical fear of Russian Communism. They were afraid Soviet armies would come bursting forth from Russia in every direction, although almost any impartial, informed man could have seen clearly that the Russians were having all they could handle at home. Unfortunately almost no one then was impartial, and very few were informed. Even the British Prime Minister Lloyd George, who remembered himself as representing as tolerant a view as could be found in Paris at the time, was frightfully alarmed at the prospect of a Germany gone Communist. On March 25, 1919, he presented to the conference a memorandum containing these passages:

> . . . Within a year we may witness the spectacle of nearly three hundred million people organized into a vast Red army under German instruction and German generals equipped with German cannon and German machine guns and prepared for a renewal of the attack on Western Europe. . . . If we are wise, we shall offer to Germany a peace, which, while just, will be preferable for all sensible men to the alternative of Bolshevism. . . . Would it (admission to the League of Nations) not be an inducement to her both to sign the terms and to resist Bolshevism? . . . Bolshevik imperialism does not merely menace the States on Russia's borders. It threatens the whole of Asia and is as near to America as it is to France.

We know now that Lloyd George and his nervous colleagues were seeing things under the bed. But at least he was frank about his fears, and they could be dealt with —as they were—by cooler heads, so far as proposals for direct intervention were concerned. But the fear of Russia had a good deal to do with modifying Allied terms in favor of Germany.

This bogey of Russia played into the hands of the German aggressors from then on. Yet the Allies had been forewarned, as we have been forewarned. As early as 1915, one of Germany's principal psychologists and philosophers, Hugo Münsterberg, wrote:

> In the perpetual striving of the nations there came one historic moment in which the two great antagonists, England and Russia, necessarily had a common wish, the

> crippling of Germany. That one common impulse brought them together for one day's common work (it took four years). But if the sun were setting over their common success, the next morning would necessarily find them the old embittered enemies. . . . Never would Germany's power be stronger than in the hour in which it had to decide whether Central Europe ought to go with England against the Russian Empire or with Russia against Great Britain. To cripple Germany means to hasten the hour in which this battle between England and Russia must be fought, and compared with that fight, the war of today may appear only as the preamble.

This is a German tune that was played with monotonous regularity—and almost as monotonous success—by the empire, the Weimar Republic and the Third Reich right up to Hitler's cry of November 12, 1944:

> Today, too, many foreign statesmen, parliamentarians and party politicians, as well as economists, have realized the necessity of saving Europe from the Bolshevik monster. Practical results, however, can be achieved only if a strong European power succeeds in organizing this common struggle for life or death, overruling all theoretical hopes, and in waging it to a successful conclusion. This can be done, and will be done, only by National Socialist Germany.

By 1944, even Hitler had worked this line too hard to command belief. But in the past it had served his turn. It brought him some of his most notable triumphs, culminating in the Munich appeasement. It failed to work at last when Russia and her present Allies joined to crush the real danger, but men with Munich minds—and they include some high in Allied councils—are as gullible as ever. Their point of view is no less dangerous to free nations now than it was in 1938, for it can destroy an essential pillar of peace, the continued co-operation of the United States, Britain and Russia.

The thoroughly effective teamwork these three have brought to bear upon the defeat of Germany has only been achieved because their governments and their people have known they all had the same aim—defeat of Germany in the shortest possible time. Victory was based on mutual confidence that all three were doing their utmost to win it. Peace is going to depend upon mutual confidence that all three mean to keep it. Obviously the minority who fear Russia, do not trust her to keep the peace. If we follow their line of building up Germany as a bulwark against Communism, Russia cannot trust us to keep the peace, for we actually will have made a start in warring upon her. Says Sumner Welles in his book, *The Time for Decision*:

> In the first postwar years the two greatest powers, both from a material as well as from a military standpoint, will be the United States and the Union of Soviet Socialist Republics. Frank recognition of this fact must underlie any consideration of the policy which this government should pursue toward the Soviet Union.
>
> The maintenance of world peace and the progress of humanity is going to depend upon the desire and the capacity of the peoples of the two countries to work together. It will depend upon their ability to replace their relationship of the past quarter of a century, which has not only been negative but marked by fanatical suspicion and deep-rooted hostility on both sides, with one that is positive and constructive.

As I have emphasized before, there are no traditional or material grounds for antagonisms between the Russian people and the people of the United States. And although only a tentative beginning has been made, the United States is the one major power, from Russia's point of view, with whom an enduring friendship should be most easily possible.

Russia can become the greatest menace that the world has yet seen. It is potentially the greatest power of the world. It can equally well become the greatest force for peace and for orderly development in the world. It is, I think, no exaggeration to say that Russia's future course depends very largely on whether the United States can persuade the Russian people and their government that their permanent and truest interest lies in cooperating with us in the creation and maintenance of a democratic and effective world organization.

It is not very persuasive nor does it help to bring about an effective world organization, to have a widely read magazine print the charge by an insignificant and disgruntled former foreign service officer of the Russian government that Communism is a growing menace to American freedom. Although the man was obscure and his knowledge of the current situation sadly out of date, an attempt to scare the reader was evident in the highly misleading heading which claimed that the article exposed the existence of a new Communist conspiracy in America. And Welles's (and America's) hope of enduring friendship with Russia will have to be strong to survive such attacks as that made by another popular magazine late in 1944. A Russian proposal for oil concessions in northern Iran was twisted into a prediction of a break in Anglo-Russian relations. The twist consisted of conjuring up a Russian plot to evade Teheran pledges and dominate Russia's neighbors.

The harm in such propaganda is not so much that we read it but that we might act upon it. Certain elements of the press have carried it on for years. Only because they are notoriously unreliable has the damage to our foreign relations been relatively slight. But it can become more serious if the same line appears in the pages of journals with a better reputation, particularly those widely read for their views on international affairs.

The test of the effectiveness of this propaganda will come in our treatment of Germany. Our Allies will rightly regard this as a much more realistic preview of our intentions than anything public men may say. If our policy is designed to buttress Germany as a bulwark against Russia, it will do more to breed another world war than any other single measure we could adopt in the whole conduct of our foreign affairs.

Advocates of this blueprint of war never advance any reasonable grounds for supposing that America really is menaced by Russia or the spread of communism. Nor do they offer any evidence for supposing that a strong Germany would protect us. All the facts point to exactly the opposite conclusion.

Ever since the United States became a country, our ideologies have been almost scurrilously antagonistic. At the same time, our relations have been not only consistently peaceful but actually friendly in the pinches. Even when one of us liked the other's form of government least, we have intervened on behalf of the people.

Although the rebellion of the thirteen colonies against King George of England seemed abominable to the Czar of Russia, the Russians nevertheless adopted a policy of armed neutrality which in practice favored the new United States. Again during our Civil War, despite a theoretical leaning toward the beliefs of the South, Russia took the stand that dismemberment of the Union would be opposed to Russian inteiests. She virtually warned England and France against recognizing the Confederacy, which they were inclined to do.

America reciprocated when Russia was being menaced by an Allied force in Siberia in 1919. The United States troops were there more for the purpose of watching the Japanese than of fighting Russians. During the course of the peace conference, both Wilson and Lloyd George went home for a short time and in their absence the conferees were whipped up to a mood of more active intervention. Wilson heard of it in mid-ocean and, although thoroughly disliking the Communistic philosophy, promptly dispatched a radio message to the effect that the only course he would agree to was speedy withdrawal of all Allied troops from Russian soil. It is the history of Russo-American relations, full of similar incidents proving our community of interests, which led Walter Lippmann to the conclusion, expressed in *U. S. Foreign Policy*:

> Historic experience shows, then, that Russia and the United States, placed "on opposite sides of the globe," have always been antagonistic in their political ideology, always suspicious that close contact would be subversive. Yet each has always opposed the dismemberment of the other. Each has always wished the other to be

strong. They have never had a collision which made them enemies. Each has regarded the other as a potential friend in the rear of its potential enemies.

No two countries have more to lose and less to gain from war. Neither competes with the other to any extent in world markets. Both are economically relatively independent of other countries. Both are rich in resources and want peace to develop them. The Russians particularly are eager to repair the enormous damage they have suffered in war and to resume that program of national development which the Western world did not really believe in until it saw the result in battle.

No, it is hardly likely that Russia will have the time or the inclination for aggression. "But," argue the fearful and the hypocritical, "we must build a bulwark against communism." Well, most Americans would rather rely upon democracy as a bulwark than upon a heavily armed Germany. And they would be right. Communism never has made much headway in this country because the people have something much better. As long as we keep it, we are in no danger from any "ism." The way to keep it is through producing in peace as we have in war. That means full employment, with everyone working to supply the whole country with all the necessities and maybe even some of the comforts and luxuries of life. It is at least as big a program as our war production has been, but we will never get it by living in fear of war and diverting our energies to building against our fear—whether we build a Maginot Line or a strong Germany.

There is no record of a democratic country going Communist. But there have been all too many examples of democracy undermined by Fascism while its people were being deluded into the belief that Communism was the real danger. Germany, Italy and Spain are the glaring instances.

If it is unreasonable to suppose that the United States is in danger from Russia or Communism, the nomination of Germany as the watchdog to guard us against peril attains fantastic heights of madness. A Bourbonism that can learn nothing from the worst war in history or from the events that led up to it is a singularly unsafe guide for any people. Yet those who propose to maintain a strong Germany as a bulwark against Russia are simply blind followers of the folly of Munich with no program for the world except the arguments, suspicions and fears of the appeasers.

The Germans are not a highly original people in the realm of ideas. We can expect them to continue to use the Communist scare which has served them so well in the past. They never lose sight of the fact that a really demilitarized, de-industrialized Reich will have no stakes with which to buy into the game of power politics. But a strong Germany could not only get into the game; she could force the rest of the world to play it no matter how much against the will of all peoples. If we build up Germany as a strong bulwark, we can expect her to play off Russia against the western Allies, offering the might of Central Europe at auction to the highest bidder. We would never be sure whether the Germans would fight with Russia against the United States or with the United States against Russia. Probably she would be fighting alone, or with such smaller satellites as she could force into her orbit through the influence of her industrial power. But certainly she would be fighting, and for world domination again. We would simply have repeated with even less excuse the most fatal blunders of the past.

"If... we are so stupid as to let Germany train and equip a large army and again become a menace to the world, we would deserve the fate which such folly would bring upon us."

So wrote the gentle and wise Colonel House in 1919. To "train and equip a large army" add the phrase "or build a strong heavy industry" and the words are as true today as we now know them to have been then. But the arguments for that colossal folly become even more significant when they are used to conceal an anti-Russian bias. Of course not all advocates of a strong postwar Germany are Red baiters. Some disagree with proposals for removing German heavy industry on grounds of mistaken humanity, but there is no concealed animosity for or fear of Russia lurking behind their arguments.

Others are not so scrupulous in presenting their motives. Unwittingly they are adopting the propaganda line most favorable to the Germans, for any return to the *cordon sanitaire* policy toward Russia is a preparation for World War III. That policy could never be imposed upon the American people openly. The attempt is being made, therefore, to lead them into this policy secretly and by way of blind alleys. Those making this attempt are proposing to dedicate the lives of our children to a purpose which they decline even to discuss with the parents. They may think their intentions are good, but good intentions make a proverbially dangerous paving, and no secret cabal ever brought anything good to this country.

If American democracy is to play its full part in winning and maintaining peace, it must be through the free play of democratic processes. That means full discussion of policies on their merits with all the arguments and all the facts before the public. For the sake of our friendship with Russia, as well as for the proper development of our own democracy, the case for and against building up Germany as a bulwark against Communism should be brought into the open. The people, whose instincts in these matters are sounder than the judgment of any cloistered "statesman," will know how to deal with it.

Chapter VIII

GERMANY HAS THE WILL TO TRY IT AGAIN

SOMETHING OVER ONE HUNDRED YEARS ago, the world outside of Germany regarded that geographical expression of dozens of states and principalities with a sentimentality, rooted in ignorance, which persists, despite all the hard lessons of history, to this day. Germany in the 1830's was a land of fairy tales where Prince Albert and Prince Ernest collected botanical specimens in the woods or played their little pianoforte duets in shabby castles, where the peasant fattened his Christmas goose in neatly tended farmyards, where most of the kings and princes of Europe found their remarkably plain wives. Of course, for centuries Europe also recruited its mercenaries from these picturesque villages. And of course the Fichtes and Hegels and Kants had been expressing the highest philosophy of these seemingly simple, peaceable, musical folk in extremely belligerent language. Only the language was so horribly dull and difficult to follow that very few outside Germany regarded it as anything more than an unpleasant academic chore.

It remained for a German to sound the warning which Europe and the world did not heed. Heinrich Heine is remembered chiefly for his love poems (and the Nazi banning of his works because of his Jewish blood) but he was also a keen observer of the contemporary scene. In

1834—it was the year a German customs union under Prussian leadership gave the first impetus to formation of the modern Germany—Heine warned France:

"You have more to fear from Germany set free than from all the Holy Alliance with its Croats and Cossacks."

Heine knew what the leaders of his people were thinking about. He knew what the teachers and philosophers were saying and writing. It would lead to "a drama compared to which the French Revolution will be only an innocent child," he thought, and although it was not beyond the realm of ideas as yet, he foresaw the reality. Referring to the then most revered German sages, he warned:

> Thought goes before the deed as lightning before the thunder. German thunder is indeed German, and not in a hurry, and it comes rolling slowly onward; but come it will, and when ye hear the crash as naught ever crashed before in the whole history of the world, then know that *der Deutsche Donner*, our German thunder, has at last hit the mark.

And again:

> It is the fairest merit of Christianity that it somewhat mitigated that brutal German *gaudium certaminis* or joy of battle, but it could not destroy it, and should that subduing talisman, the Cross, break, then will come crashing and roaring forth the wild madness of the old champions, the insane berserker rage of which Northern poets say and sing. That talisman is brittle, and the day will come when it will pitifully break. The old stone gods will rise from long forgotten ruin, and rub the dust of a thousand years from their eyes, and

Thor, leaping to life with his giant hammer, will smash the Gothic cathedrals!

The poet drew this remarkably accurate prophecy from his reading of the German mind quite as much as from his reading of the German philosophers. But for one hundred years Germans in Germany have preferred Hegel to Heine. Anyone who has tried both will understand why the German taste appears too mysterious to others, why a greater German even than Heine was dismayed by the paradox in the native character as he saw it.

"I have often felt a bitter pang," wrote Goethe, "at the thought of the German people, so estimable as individuals and so wretched in the whole."

The reason was that Germans were not so much uneducated as they were elaborately and deliberately miseducated. The medieval belief that war was not only the sole profession fit for a gentleman but that it was also the best trade for a common fellow survived in Germany long after it had been outmoded in all the rest of Europe that passed for civilized. It survives today. To that belief was added and is still added a sedulously fostered conviction that the German is not only a better man than any foreigner—other peoples have indulged the same conceit—but that the German is destined to rule over the inferior people, too. The conception of that rule as a civilizing mission was notable by its absence. Germany was to dominate the world with lash and club for the sole comfort and enrichment of Germans.

Of course other nations have had their share of megalomaniacs. Glorification of war for its own sake, theories of a master race, the blasphemy that God made some peoples as servants for others have cropped up in the writings of almost every country. But outside Germany they were confined to a little-heeded minority, a lunatic fringe. Inside Germany, the same teachings were if anything more lunatic, and they were also official, all-pervading and finally accepted without question.

The Nazis pushed these theories further in practice than any of their predecessors, but they could not have done it without the generations of preparation. The German people had to be cultivated intensively for nearly two hundred years before they could produce those finest Nazi flowers—the gas chambers of Maidaneck and the massacre of Lidice. It would be a highly reckless gamble to act on the wishful thought that the blood of nearly six years of war has not only fertilized this soil but changed its character. For the traditional German will to war goes back as far as our own traditional will to freedom.

While Americans were debating the rival political philosophies of Jefferson and Hamilton, and deciding that they preferred the greater promise of democracy, Germans were reading a complete preview of the Nazi regime. It was 1800 and the United States was enjoying the hottest presidential campaign of the new century, but Johann Gottlieb Fichte had just anticipated Hjalmar Schacht with a book called *The Closed Commercial State*. Briefly his program called for a planned economy, barter trade with other countries, blocked currency, concealed inflation, ersatz materials. The objective was *Lebensraum*, and to get this German living space, Fichte called for intensive armaments, the occupation of desirable territory and the transfer of populations. In a Europe dominated by

Napoleon, this could be confused with patriotism, but it did not die with the French dictator.

In the next generation, while the British people were concerned with no political subject so much as the Reform Bill, which finally passed in 1832, Germans were studying Hegel. This paladin of German philosophy taught that the state was the most perfect manifestation of God in the world of men; that the Prussian state was the noblest expression of that heavenly mandate, and that its emergence was the culmination of the historical process.

During this period and for many years afterward, the German people's resources for war and conquest were ridiculously inadequate to the grandiose tasks for which they were being prepared. France, England, Russia, Austria were the big powers, and even Prussia could not at the time be considered in the first rank. But German teachers continued to preach a gospel of war and racial superiority. As Heine said, they were in no hurry. About the middle of the century one of the Germans whose words were most widely quoted was Johann Wappaus, a geographer. He was instilling into the German people a belief that the Latin, Negro and Indian races were quite incapable of any sustained effort unless driven to it by their superiors "through the weight of an iron will or the foreman's lash." Wappaus left no doubt that both the will and the lash should be German.

By 1862 the means for conquest were beginning to bear some proportion to the German lust for it. The first seizures of territory were to begin in two years, and one of the earliest German "Big Navy" advocates, J. J. Sturz, put out a popular book in which he made the lordly assumption, apparently shared by his readers, that territorial aggrandizement by Germany was a law of nature. The seizure of Schleswig-Holstein after a short war with Denmark in 1864, seemed to Germans to confirm this point of view. If further proof was needed, it was supplied by the Six Weeks War of 1866, by which Austria was ousted from her leadership among German states, and the Franco-Prussian War of 1870, which added Alsace-Lorraine to a new German Empire.

Germany was suddenly the most powerful nation in Europe, and the education of her people in their self-assigned role of master race was stimulated through all possible media of propaganda. The schools were mobilized from kindergarten to university; books and magazines were dedicated to the proposition that Germans loved war and were destined to rule the world; public figures proclaimed the beauties of German domination over lesser tribes, and in 1890 the Pan-German movement was launched to foster more systematically the ideas of territorial expansion and world conquest. As early as 1893, one of its publications, prophetically entitled *Greater Germany and Central Europe Approximately in 1940*, trumpeted:

> Germans alone will govern . . . they alone will exercise political rights; they alone will serve in the army and in the navy; they alone will have the right to become land-owners; thus they will acquire the conviction that, as in the Middle Ages, the Germans are a people of rulers. However, they will condescend so far as to delegate inferior tasks to foreign subjects who live among them.

Five years later, when The Hague Conference was groping vainly for a formula for peace and disarmament, the Pan-German magazine *Heimdall* was objecting:

"For us Germans the abolition of war can become possible only—if at all—when the German Reich, that is, the Pan-German Reich in the widest sense, has become the Super-State, the supreme power, in the world."

As a new century was ushered in, most peoples of the world were hoping it would be one of profound peace. But the German Admiral von Tirpitz was talking earnestly about the possibility of seizing a naval base for Germany in the Caribbean. The Pan-German leader, Dr. Wintzer, spoke about protecting the interests of Germans overseas, referred magniloquently to "the universal mission of the German race" and demanded that Germans everywhere recognize their "duty to work for a policy of systematic expansion."

From this time until 1914, Germany was carrying on a war of nerves—although the term had not yet been invented—to the tune of pretty general applause from her people. They thrilled to their bellicose Kaiser Wilhelm when in a speech at Tangier in 1905, while using French claims to Morocco as a sounding board for aggressive German designs, he cried:

"We are the salt of the earth . . . God has created us so that we should civilize the world."

Germans thought he meant by that what Professor Ernest Hasse wrote in his *The German Reich as a National State*, published that same year:

> Who, in the future, is to do the heavy and dirty work which every national community based on labor will

> always need? . . . The solution consists in our condemning alien European stock, the Poles, Czechs, Jews, Italians and so on, who live under us, or find their way to us, to these slaves' conceptions.

The history of German aggression in these years was a blend of action and propaganda. When the Kaiser was bringing on the Moroccan crisis of 1911 and extorting a slice of the Congo from France as the price of refraining from war over a settlement he had agreed to in 1906, German fondness for war was being stimulated by the printed page. General von Bernhardt strategically brought out a new book called *Germany and the Next War* in which Berlin was stirred to a strong support of the possible conflict over Morocco.

"Our people must learn that the preservation of peace cannot and must never be the aim of our policy," he wrote, and: "War is not only a necessary element in the life of peoples, but also the indispensable factor in culture, indeed the highest expression of the strength and life of truly cultural peoples."

As World War I drew nearer, the glorification of war and contempt for other peoples grew even more blatant. Two examples from 1913 give the tone of innumerable speeches and articles of the time.

"War is the noblest and holiest expression of German activity," proclaimed the October issue of *Jungdeutschland*, a magazine for German youth of Boy Scout age. " . . . Let us ridicule to the utmost the old women in breeches who fear war and deplore it as cruel and revolting. No, war is beautiful. Its august sublimity elevates the human heart beyond the earthly and the common."

"The historical view as to the biological evolution of races tells us that there are dominant races and subordinate races," explained the Pan-German organ, *Alldeutsche Blaetter*, " . . . Conquest in particular is always a function of the dominant races. . . . The conquerors are acting only according to biological principles if they suppress alien languages and undertake to destroy strange popular customs. . . . Only the conquering race must be populous, so that it can overrun the territory it has won."

When war came, the arrogance of the Kaiser was hardly to be distinguished from that of Hitler a quarter of a century later, except that Wilhelm's effusions were couched in somewhat better grammar. Representative of four years of imperial rabble rousing was this proclamation to the Armies of the East in 1914:

"Remember that you are the chosen people! The spirit of the Lord has descended upon me, because I am Emperor of the Germans! I am the instrument of the Most High. I am His sword, His representative. . . . May all the enemies of the German people perish! God demands their destruction, God, who through my mouth, commands you to execute His will."

Wilhelm was not uniquely mad, as many readers in Allied lands supposed from reading his proclamations. Heinrich von Treitschke was considered the chief living German historian. What his science had taught him, he wrote in 1916, was "that war is both justifiable and moral, and that the ideal of perpetual peace is not only impossible but immoral as well . . . Anyone with a knowledge of history realizes that to expel war from the universe would be to mutilate German freedom. . . . War must be conceived as an institution ordained by God." Nor was this a war-induced hysteria. Twenty years before, in the midst of peace, Treitschke had remarked that "those who preach the nonsense of eternal peace do not understand Aryan national life."

After 1918, it seemed impossible to the victors that the vanquished could take seriously the sort of rhetoric their Kaiser and their sages had dished out to them. But an idea cannot be beaten by a battle. There is no common meeting ground for conflict. An idea needs to be beaten by another idea, and their military defeat had given birth to no new ideas among the Germans. Mere loss of a war, especially one in which they had held the field for years against a coalition of all the chief powers of the world, did not seem to Germans any reason for doubting the truth of Fichte and Hegel, Treitschke and the Kaiser. They were inclined to remember—and their orators, writers and teachers reminded them—how close they had been to victory. They had missed taking Paris in 1914 by sheer bad luck, the German version runs, and the men of the Weimar Republic could reflect wistfully on the glories that might have been if the French capital had succumbed. If Oswald Spengler, the philosopher author of *The Decline of the West*, could learn nothing from defeat, how could the world reasonably expect average citizens to unlearn two or three lifetimes of miseducation? And Spengler could write in 1921:

"A genuine international is only possible through the victory of the idea of *one* race over all others . . . we Germans . . . have rich unspent possibilities within us and huge tasks before us . . . The real international is imperialism."

The most notable figure in German official life who was believed to have been converted to democracy and peace between the two wars was Gustav Stresemann. His most sympathetic biographer says of him:

"His first creed . . . was force . . . With his belief in power went a belief in authority . . . Combined with Stresemann's belief in power and authority was a belief in discipline."

So Stresemann supported the war of 1914 with enthusiasm, urged unlimited U-boat warfare with all his might and saw the overthrow of the empire with indignation. Yet he was no Junker militarist. He was the son of a restaurant keeper, the product of German universities, and he looked like an unfriendly caricature of the German middle class. After the war, he led the political party which was financed by Hugo Stinnes, the Ruhr industrialist. His only differences with the financier arose over Stresemann's insistence that the state was bigger than business.

"German industry should not be regarded as an end in itself, but as a means to an end," he wrote.

Stresemann, who was Chancellor when Hitler staged his beer hall putsch on November 8, 1923, saw that Germany needed to be reconciled to the European family of nations to speed her recovery. As Foreign Minister, he developed a real belief in peace, and it was he who signed Locarno. The treaty was hailed with rapture in all the signatory countries but one. Germany was so indignant with the acceptance of Alsace-Lorraine's permanent loss that

Stresemann had to be smuggled back into Berlin obscurely under police guard to save his life. Even when he negotiated the evacuation of the Rhineland five years ahead of time, there was more outcry in Germany against his failure to abolish reparations than praise for his success. His biographer reports that as he read the newspaper attacks just before his death, he cried:

"It is madness." And added after a moment: "Then I have lived in vain."

Of all his generation, Stresemann made the biggest effort to weaken his country's will to war. He won more prestige abroad than any other German public man between the two wars; he had and used unrivaled eloquence; he was one of the shrewdest and ablest of politicians; he had the advantages of his early powerful backing by Stinnes, his own belligerent war record and his diplomatic triumphs. But not even his biographer thinks he made any impression on German thought or long-range German policy. He was used as a tool to win concessions Germany was still too weak to force. But he won no German converts to conciliation.

Since Stresemann died, the German people have been subjected to a more sustained program for strengthening the will to war than he could have imagined. For twelve years the whole force of the most highly organized propaganda machine in history has played upon the German mind, already well prepared to receive it. Contrary points of view have been silenced with unusual ferocity and also with unusual thoroughness. Defeat by the United Nations has brought no visible signs that the German dream of conquest had faded any more than it did in 1918. Hitler himself realized that this would be true when, fresh from the seizure of Austria and the Sudetenland in 1938, he was quoted as saying:

> A defeated nation can even better than a victorious nation be trained and prepared for the day of final victory. It may happen that I cannot win victory at once in this coming war; we may be forced to interrupt it. Then we will all be back underground. But after some years, when the weak and inefficient democracies will have utterly failed to solve the world's postwar problems, then we will suddenly break loose from underground and our stupefied enemies will discover all too late that millions of their own youth, misguided by weak education, disappointed by democracy's failure, will be on our side. Victory in this Third World War will be quick and easy.

American observers who have entered captured German towns find no weakening of the German will. It is as strong today as was Hitler's in 1938. Its persistence is reflected in the woman of Aachen, quoted in the New York *Times*. Indicating the burning city she said:

"If the British had only surrendered in 1940, none of this would have happened."

Inevitably Germans will remember much more clearly how close they came to victory than how they came to be defeated. But even if they had not come so close, the will which has supported two world wars with terrible tenacity and virtual unanimity will not be broken by a few disasters. Desire for war has been as firmly planted in the German as desire for freedom in the American. The process has been going on in both for about the same length of time. Few people would suggest that the German is the less stubborn of the two. Yet how many decades would a conqueror need to kill the spark of freedom in America? Optimists may hope that the extinction of Germany's lust for war could be accomplished in no longer a period. But if they are realists, too, they will not take a chance that it can be done any more quickly.

Chapter IX

GERMANY HAS THE MEANS TO TRY IT AGAIN

EVERY PROPOSAL SAVE ONE FOR blocking a new German war effort is predicated on the theory that Germany either hasn't really any will to war—it was all just a couple of mistakes—or else that the German will to war is so weak that it can be eradicated by one method or another before it has a chance to do any more harm. The one plan for peace which does not rest on any such shaky foundation is to deprive Germany of the power to wage effective modern war. The simple logic of this formula runs about as follows:

If Germany does not want to start another war in twenty or thirty years, it will be small hardship to deprive her of the means of doing so.

If Germany does want to start another war, no hardships that might prevent it would be too severe to impose.

In either case, Germany and the world will be a great deal safer and happier if the Reich loses her war potential.

She has not lost it yet. The vivid descriptions of the devastation wrought by Allied bombing and shelling served to obscure rather than paint the true picture. Miles of rubble and the twisted skeletons of buildings not quite leveled may be the appropriate tombstone of the Hitlerian madness. But they are not proof of German heavy industry's death. The bombs and shells made no more than a start on the job of destroying that; the Allies must complete the task with a thoroughness which should take no account of the momentary convenience of occupying authorities.

That this will require some very specific orders to the Army is clear from the experience of the first months of occupation and even the last months of war. Partial surveys of German industrial capacity show that a surprisingly large number of factories were damaged only superficially while many were entirely unscathed. Some of these latter apparently owed their escape to the careful, precise work of Allied airmen. Among them were the Ford and Courtauld plants at Cologne. They shared the immunity of the famous cathedral. General Motors' Opel works were said to be almost the only buildings intact in Russelsheim, and by June trucks were being turned out there for our Army.

The seemingly miraculous escape of the I. G. Farben works at Hoechst brought forth two explanations. London's *New Statesman* noted that American firms had been associated in the enterprise before the war. The New York *Times* reported that the Allies had been tricked by information received through Switzerland to the effect that the plant produced only medicine, although actually it was 40 per cent in war work. Whatever the reason, this sprawling colossus—it employed 12,000 workers—was known to be so safe that the people of Hoechst used it as an air-raid shelter.

Among the most modern and efficient German factories were about one hundred which literally went underground to escape bombing. These are untouched, although they offer a unique opportunity for an experiment in the genuine disarmament of Germany. If the subterranean workshops were filled to capacity with German war equipment and blown up, the world would know that we mean to deal severely with the German war potential.

Instead, according to the London *Statist* of June 30, there were four hundred factories operating in the Ruhr, Rhineland and Saar alone. Other sources noted that the great majority of plants were not far from normal working conditions, so that it was said Germany on her surrender retained 75 per cent of her industrial capacity. A representative survey taken in the United States zone of occupation shows why. The forty-five plants covered were listed as follows:

Completely destroyed	3
More than half destroyed	10
50 per cent to 60 per cent usable	1
70 per cent to 80 per cent usable	8
80 per cent to 90 per cent usable	5
90 per cent to 100 per cent usable	18

Thus Germany remains the genuine "have" country from a strictly military point of view. France, Holland, Belgium, Poland, Yugoslavia and even England are the "have nots" in the topsy-turvy bookkeeping of Mars.

The concept of Germany as the real seat of modern imperial power as compared to "have not" Britain and France takes some getting used to. But looked at clearly and solely in the light of total war, without any mitigating sentimentality about the welfare of individuals or the sanctity of life, heavy industry can more than make up for any shortage of raw material that a really determined belligerent would need.

Germany proved that conclusively. In the winter of 1939-1940, the period of the so-called "phony" war, we heard very positive, detailed explanations of how shortages must soon cause the Reich's collapse. The Allies, it was said, were so rich in raw materials that they would be able to starve out an encircled Germany, even though the Nazis could call on the resources of eastern and Central Europe. For there was only Rumanian oil, not enough to support a real war. There was no rubber, a scarcity of many important alloy metals, a lack of tropical products of all kinds.

The armchair strategists forgot that raw materials are usable only after they have been fabricated. But the heavy industries can use the most unlikely raw materials. The ability of chemical industries to supply almost any quantity of synthetics has been proved by the fact that in more than five years of a far tougher war than anyone in 1939 anticipated, the Wehrmacht right up to the end was not fatally short of any of the things that were supposed to destroy her by their absence. Part of it, of course, was due to enormous stockpiles gathered in the years before the war. Another part was due to the speedy conquest of some sources of raw materials. But mainly, the reliance has been upon the products of German heavy industry. That heavy industry still has the highest capacity in Europe except as it may have been distanced in a few particulars by the Russians.

Therefore, Germany remains potentially the strongest military nation in Europe except perhaps Russia. Five years of totalitarian control over most of the continent, added to years of economic warfare against other European industry, have left the Reich even stronger in defeat, compared to her neighbors, than she was in victory. Yet even before the war, Germany led the world in chemicals and was second only to the United States in iron and steel production, fabricating of steel, machine tools, capacity for the manufacture of electrical equipment. These were the basis for the amazing striking power of her blitzkrieg. For them, and for them alone, even the ingenuity of war and the magic of science have found no substitutes.

The actual number of men under arms is not a very important consideration in war, and never was in spite of the rather impious military proverb about God being on the side of the stronger battalions. History is full of the defeat of mere numbers who were not so well equipped or so well trained as their enemies. Other things being equal, equipment was always decisive.

There is a little story about the great English host that waited in the camp at Tilbury in 1588 for the Spanish Army that was to cross the Channel as soon as the Invincible Armada had cleared England's insignificant little Navy out of the way. The Army never got its chance, of course, because Drake's few ships were a more powerful striking weapon than the hundreds of clumsy Spanish antiques. But the energetic Queen Elizabeth and her nobles had gathered at Tilbury a great many more soldiers than King Philip's commander could ferry across the water. Elizabeth herself reviewed the troops with a captain of the House of de Vere at her side. De Vere had seen a great deal of the Spanish Army in action, and he knew very well the quality of Spanish weapons, for Spain in that age was to warlike nations what Germany has been in ours. He watched his countrymen brandishing their homemade pikes and looked very gloomy as he wondered what Spanish firearms would do to those close-packed ranks. He was the only experienced soldier and the only obviously unhappy man near the Queen that day, and she pressed him for an explanation.

"Madam," he replied, "Your Grace's Army is brave indeed. I have not in the world the name of a coward, and yet I am the greatest coward here. All these fine fellows are praying that the enemy may land, and that there may be a battle. And I, who know that enemy well, cannot think of such a battle without dismay."

The more recent the examples, the more striking they are, for the products of heavy industry increasingly outweigh valor and numbers. The French Army in 1940 was larger than the German Army. It collapsed in a little more than a month. The Czech, Polish and Yugoslav armies were each larger than the combined forces of the British Empire before the war broke out. Of them all, only Britain gave the German war machine any trouble. In large part that was because England was nearer a match for the Reich in heavy industry than any of her opponents up to that time. Britain could convert to war fast enough—and barely fast enough—to hold the fort until the strength of the United States was mobilized.

That strength lay in the steel mills of Pittsburgh and Birmingham, the assembly lines of Michigan and California, the machine tool factories of Vermont and Ohio, the chemical works of Wilmington and Chicago, the shipyards east, west and south, the turbine plants of Schenectady and Bridgeport, the immense power of TVA, Boulder and Shasta, and so on through the mighty catalogue of heavy industry.

Bataan proved to anyone who needed proof that courage is no adequate retort to planes and tanks and heavy artillery. A thousand battles on the road back from the defeats of 1941 and 1942 have proved that it is heavy industry which arms courage for victory. Against a modern enemy, nothing else can.

So the Germans will retain, if they retain heavy industry, all that they will need to launch another war in twenty or thirty years. They had to wait twenty-one years after their previous defeat to build the arsenal they thought they needed to overrun the world. With the ever-increasing tempo of modern industry, it should not take them longer, if so long, next time.

The German lust for war survived defeat in 1918, and was intensified by skillful propaganda and wild demagogy. But the yearning for revenge, the myriad illegal military organizations, the intensive search for new and improved weapons, the fifth column work among intended victims—the whole scheme of German aggression would have had to dissipate itself in empty mouthings and ridiculous parades if it had not been equipped by German heavy industry. Hitler must have remained a figure of fun if it had not been for Krupp and Thyssen and Hugenberg. Heavy industry alone permitted a man born for slapstick comedy to convert himself into Wagnerian tragedy.

The real failure of the Versailles Treaty was that its authors did not recognize the true wellsprings of military force when they saw them. They had not had our doubtful advantages in this respect. They had the rather common delusion that hard work would be a good thing for the German people, taking their minds off war and enabling them to pay for some of the damage they had done. It seemed quite fitting that Germans should delve in coal mines and sweat at blast furnaces to supply the victims of their aggression.

Of course it did not work out that way. (Why should we think that it would work that way now?) The Germans did not even wait for the peace treaty to be ratified before they were preparing to scuttle those provisions of it which seriously interfered with their plans for another war. Those plans were based upon German supremacy in metals and metal products, in chemicals, in machinery of all kinds. Once they had that, they had supremacy in arms any time they wanted to convert to military purposes.

At least as early as 1920, the year the Versailles Treaty was ratified, the German industrialists began their campaign of building up heavy industries, using funds held abroad so that they escaped seizure and combining among themselves for bigger mergers. Typical of them, and one of the first, since it was organized in 1919, was the octopus-like I. G. Farben (*Interessengemeinschaft Farbenindustrie Aktien Gesellschaft*, to give it its full, seldom-used name), which was soon to get back the patents seized by the United States during World War I. The president of the new colossus was Karl Bosch, inventor of chlorine poison gas, and the chairman was Karl Duisberg, the principal developer of ersatz products in Germany up to that time.

This and other combines had mapped out a program

of reconstruction and expansion for their factories even before the defeated German troops had been demobilized. Their plans were under the supervision of the clandestine general staff, but the first task was simply to outbuild Europe in all heavy industry without worrying about specific application to war uses. Both the general staff and the German industrialists knew that conversion to war was a relatively easy matter once industrial capacity was achieved.

The transfer of Lorraine with its iron ore to France had been thought by the conferees at Paris in 1919 to cut the German iron and steel industry down to size. But by 1929, blast furnace capacity within the smaller Reich had increased 70-80 per cent; steelmaking capacity by 25 per cent, and rolling mill capacity by 11 per cent. The National Industrial Conference Board reported that by 1931 Germany was "ready to challenge the United States on its favorite ground of large scale production . . . the iron and steel industry of Germany is better equipped for efficient production than that of any other European country and is not much behind the United States." Yet in 1931, it was commonly supposed that Germany was powerless against such a great military nation as France and would probably be unable to resist Poland.

A further blow to German industry in general was expected in 1919 to follow cession of rich German coal areas to France and Poland. Ten years later, in her smaller territory, Germany was producing 15 per cent more coal than she had in the war-hungry year of 1918. Yet that was not taken as an alarm signal.

All in all, Germany rose during the twenties to second

place in world manufacturing capacity, behind only the United States. Within six years of the Armistice, her chemical industry was 25 per cent greater than in 1914. In ten years from the end of the war, her electro-technical industry expanded production by 70 per cent.

All this, theoretically, was for civilian use. But it did not take long for the military to co-ordinate this civilian production. Machine tools are, as the United States found in 1940, the key to conversion of peaceful industry to war work. The Germans after 1918 saw without very much sorrow their obsolescent machine tools taken from the munitions plants and shipped to the Allies. The victors were stuck with them; the vanquished built new, better ones. As early as 1924, the German government took a census of machine tools then in existence. From that date, all specifications for new machine tools had to be submitted to the Reichswehr so that the Army could be sure they were suitable for military purposes when the moment came to use them. The industry was expanded rapidly, until it too ranked second only to that of the United States.

Side by side with the development of heavy industry and as an indispensable part of that development, Germany expanded her industrial research facilities. Science was at work in factories all over the world, but in Germany it was virtually in the Army. Technical progress was directed by the general staff in great measure, and research for war was pursued under the guise of peace when that was necessary and quite openly when concealment ceased to be important.

All of that was ready to Hitler's hand years before he

came to power. The Weimar Republic had saved the real strength of imperial Germany for the use of the Third Reich. It was this contribution to the cause of war to which one of the supposedly democratic leaders of the republic referred when he claimed more credit than Hitler for the armed power which the Nazis wielded. Dr. Karl Joseph Wirth, who had been Chancellor in 1921, was quoted in a newspaper interview of 1937 as saying:

"As to the rearmament of Germany, Hitler has only continued the rearmament that had been prepared by the Weimar Republic. I, myself, deserve great credit for this preparation. . . . The real reorganization was our work."

When Hitler became the master of Germany in 1933, he had, therefore, the basis for his Wehrmacht. In the eyes of the world Germany was still disarmed. Six years later, she was not alone in thinking herself invincible.

Our own transformation from peace to a war footing took place even more rapidly than Germany's. With less advance planning but with greater resources in the real machinery of war, the United States in four years far surpassed Germany's achievement in six. Most of our great war production record was made in the factories which in 1939 had turned out 7,000,000 trucks and automobiles, 2,000,000 electric refrigerators, 1,500,000 washing machines, 1,000,000 vacuum cleaners and all the other items by which a peaceful nation shows its strength.

As long as Germany has the capacity for turning out ships, locomotives, automobiles, tractors, dynamos, transport planes, steel rails, nitrates, dyes, synthetics, machine tools and so on, she has the power to wage a long and bloody war. The first time she tried it, she did not miss by much. The second time she came so close to victory that most of the world is frightened yet. A third time the peaceful peoples might not be even so fortunate as to regain and maintain their freedom at the cost of twenty million dead and half the earth ravaged. German heavy industry will hang over humanity as an ever-present threat as long as it is permitted to exist.

They say that there are close analogies between the human body and the body politic. We know that if a limb is not used, it atrophies. That may be true with nations. If the German will to fight is not exercised, it may die. If the German sword arm, which is heavy industry, is not used at all, the German people may get quite out of the habit of aggression. They may even lose their taste for it. That would seem to be a more intelligent treatment than to hand over anvil, hammer and iron and suggest that something new be forged. The something new might conceivably be a plowshare, but it is far more likely to be a sword.

Certainly it is the treatment we would be demanding if we had learned anything from the history of our own times. We know that the most advanced metallurgical industry in Europe made possible the Panzer divisions which crushed a dozen peaceful peoples. We know that the electrical industry made possible the Luftwaffe and its career of destruction and terror. We know that the chemical industries made possible the lethal chambers of Maidaneck. We cannot afford to say, therefore, that we deplore Maidaneck, that we condemn the Luftwaffe, that we abhor the Panzers but that we are perfectly willing to have the German industries which created them remain to do it again.

Chapter X

GERMANY AND DEMOCRACY

ON A DAMP, FOGGY NIGHT A LITTLE more than twenty years ago, the Weimar Republic gave perhaps its most perfect demonstration of what Germans understand democracy to mean. The incident explains at once why it was so easy to indoctrinate them with contempt for the very idea of political freedom and why the peace of the world can never be safe in the presence of anything such a people might consider a democratic form of government.

It was November 8, 1923, and a raw wind blew like a wet dishcloth against the faces of Cabinet Ministers hurrying to an emergency meeting in the Chancellery. For nearly five years these men and their like—Social Democrats, Socialists, Centrists, the so-called democratic party leaders—had been in nominal control of the government. They were used to crises. They had seen the mark speeding on its disastrous course of inflation. They had seen the occupation of the Ruhr. They had been through the political battles of a succession of coalition Cabinets.

On this November night, however, the leaders of the republic were in a remarkable state of funk. A demagogue named Adolf Hitler was trying to start a revolution in a beer hall. The story in Berlin that evening was that his movement had captured Bavaria and was marching on the national capital. To do the Cabinet Ministers justice, they were a good deal more frightened by the fact that General Erich Ludendorff of World War fame had joined the little Austrian. And they were frightened most of all by worry over which way the Army would jump.

The figureheads of the republic knew that the Army had no love for them. It was in the hands of the old military clique, the Prussian war lords whose destruction had been promised by the Allies. Within five years of their supposed demise, they had become the power that would decide whether the republic survived. If the soldiers, carefully trained in anti-republican dogma, preferred the Hitlerian raincoat to the parliamentary frock coat, the Weimar regime was doomed.

The finest elements of that regime sat in a big, dimly lit room in the Chancellery. In the confusion of calling the hasty meeting, someone had forgotten to turn on all the lights, and one of the participants in the gathering later remembered that the members of the Cabinet already looked like ghosts. President Ebert, who seemed an old man although he was only fifty-two, paced the floor. His latest Chancellor, the bull-necked Stresemann, sat back in a chair reporting to his colleagues in a voice which some of them thought he strained to keep steady. But these men were not looking to the people to protect their republic. Apparently not one of them in this crisis even so much as thought that their power derived from the masses about whom they talked so glibly in the Reichstag; certainly not one of them proposed that the real sovereign in any democracy be consulted.

Instead, as Stresemann finished talking, they turned

anxiously to the one man in that room who hardly paid even lip service to such a thing as a republic, let alone democracy. General Hans von Seeckt, tall and slim in his neat, tight-fitting field gray, crossed one leg over the other and swung an elegantly shod foot while a beam of light reflected blankly from the still circle of his monocle. His companions were horribly nervous, but he was impassive. As commander of the treaty army, he represented to these uneasy republicans the true source of authority. At last Ebert broke the long silence, demanding in a noticeably hoarse voice:

"And the Reichswehr, Herr General, will they stick to the Reich or go over to Bavaria?"

"The Reichswehr," replied the real master of Germany, "will stick to me, Herr President."

Before the Ministers left the room, General von Seeckt had been entrusted with a virtual dictatorship. He issued a few short words of command, and the beer hall putsch collapsed. The military and their allies, the industrialists, were not yet ready for a Hitler. The republic was said to have been saved.

Actually, of course, the republic was merely a disguise behind which the generals and the Ruhr magnates found it easy to operate. The very fact that the republic allowed itself to be so used was an added reason why the German people regarded it with contempt. A sham democracy which rushed for shelter to the protection of its worst enemies was hardly a sight to inspire enthusiasm for democratic ideals. Neither the Germans nor their leaders —nor apparently foreigners who dream wistfully of a regenerated Reich—understand that a democratic government is the expression of a people; the people never become a democracy because a little group of rulers tells them they are one. The omelet, in short, is made from the eggs, but not even modern scientific magic has discovered a way to make eggs out of an omelet.

Germany now finds herself in much the same position, so far as democracy is concerned, as in 1918 but with the conditions aggravated many times over. Her defeat has been more complete and more devastating than before. Her own land bears the terrible open wounds of war, as it did not in 1918. Her people have been much more elaborately miseducated for freedom and common decency. They face a much more difficult task of reconversion and reconstruction, a much more disastrous period of poverty and hunger. They are hated with a virulence unknown in modern times because it has never been so richly deserved.

Any government that has to deal with a people in this situation is going to be extremely unpopular. If it takes a democratic form, it is going to labor under the additional handicap of ingrained German dislike. The test of any German's fitness for public office under Allied occupation should not be so much his sentiments, but whether or not he is likely to help lead his community and his country away from their desire to rebuild heavy industry's war potential.

This, even more than the pro-Nazi records of individuals selected for key posts, can be a danger. It is a danger that apparently was overlooked or minimized in the first months of Allied occupation. Even where it was recognized at the top, it was neglected by minor officials. Ample evidence of this accumulated rapidly. Not only was the reconstruction of industries turned over to the management which had served the Nazis, but public and financial posts were bestowed by American officers upon Germans who perhaps had not been active party members but had collaborated with and prospered under the Third Reich. The same thing has been noted by British officers in their zone of occupation.

Representative of many lesser selections, was the choice of Friedrich Schaeffer as Minister President of Bavaria. The choice was made by Colonel Charles E. Keegan, the American military government official, and it roused a good deal of adverse comment at the time. Most of the objections to Schaeffer were made on the ground of his reactionary past rather than active collaboration with the Nazis, since he actually had been jailed by them and held for a time in Dachau. The real peril in the Schaeffer appointment is that he is identified in the mind of Germans with that democratic philosophy they have been taught to despise. Hardly anyone outside Germany, certainly no one in any really democratic country would regard Schaeffer, who in his time was a political ally of the industrialists and most backward clerical elements in Bavaria, as a representative of democracy. But it is not the democratic peoples elsewhere so much as the Germans we have to consider. To them Schaeffer and his kind are reminders of the Weimar Republic's failures—a symbol of what many of them distrust in democracy.

The groups to which these men belonged once served as a cloak for the war plans of the Junkers and the chiefs of heavy industry who were the real masters of Germany. To put them back in power or even the semblance of power is to discredit genuine democracy far more than would the nomination of actual Nazis. The same forces that undermined the Weimar Republic would operate, intensified by the recollection of how it was done twenty years ago. The United Nations should not permit that bit of history to repeat itself.

The republic, and what Germans said was democracy, were blamed then for unemployment, reparations, the occupation by Allied troops, riots, inflation, assassinations, shortages—all the evils that descend upon a defeated people. Dislike of the Weimar regime was cleverly fostered by propaganda. Even if the republic itself had not been so much the creature of its enemies, it would have become distasteful to Germans before long.

The quirks that democratic shams took in Germany seemed to the world of the long armistice to be rather amusing, although a few recognized them as dangerous. It is important that we understand the danger this time, and be ready to meet it. When Field Marshal von Hindenburg was elected President—the only man the Germans ever did elect to that post, for Ebert was the product of a national assembly—it seemed faintly ridiculous that a democratic republic should elect an old Junker who disapproved of republics and would take the job only after asking his former imperial master for permission. What failed to register then, and has not registered with many yet, is that it would have been more than ridiculous; it would have been impossible, if the republic really had been democratic.

It seemed funny, too, when the Nazis in spite of their loud contempt for democratic parliaments competed eagerly for seats in the Reichstag. It was laughable that these men thought as much of the salaries of deputies and the free railroad tickets as they did of political influence which membership might give. It was not taken seriously when Goebbels wrote in *Der Angriff*:

> We enter Parliament in order to supply ourselves in the arsenal of democracy, with its own weapons, to paralyze the Weimar sentiment with its own assistance. If democracy is so stupid as to give us free tickets and salaries for this purpose, that is its affair.

The Nazis no longer seem very funny. The bad farce turned into real tragedy. It was a tragedy for democracy even more than for the German people. They, after all, got what they wanted. One reason they got it was that the democratic form of Germany's government blinded the world to the real peril behind it during just those years when the memory of the war might have made even England and America a little suspicious.

Suspicion of Germany's "democracy" would have been justified whether democracy is considered as merely the machinery of administration or as a way of life. In either case, it reflects the will of the people, and certainly the German governments between the two world wars did that. The fact that it was a belligerent will is worth remembering. After all, Germany is not the first nation that has had aggressive designs. Americans like to regard themselves and the British as the most advanced exponents of the democratic process. Under somewhat different forms, both governments are and must be responsive to the will of the people. But both have turned to conquest. The British did not acquire their empire in a fit of absentmindedness or without employing armed force against other peoples. The United States did not become a great continental power possessed of certain islands overseas without picking a few fights. Our wars with Mexico and Spain were certainly not carried on against the will of the people; both roused rather extensive enthusiasm. The fact that we hope we have learned better by now should not blind us to the historical fact that a desire for war is not incompatible with a democratic form of government.

Democracy as a way of life is another matter. The idea of a government responsible to the people and obliged to obtain a fresh mandate from the people at regular intervals has broadened out into something a great deal more important but not quite so easily described. Democracy to most Americans and most Englishmen has a certain set of human values quite distinct from elections, terms of office, powers of the Executive and so on. We live by, or at least sincerely try to live by a set of freedoms and responsibilities. The rights of individuals come first with us—the right to talk and eat and write and worship as we please, the right to earn a living at anything our abilities fit us for, the right to go where we want and leave when we please. As a corollary, we believe that other individuals have the same rights and that force as an instrument of national policy is to be abhorred.

The hallmark of democracy in this sense is that even when it is not altogether observed, the people who violate its tenets feel called upon to justify themselves. They do not deny the validity of the ideal; they say that the circumstances under which they are living at the moment do not permit them to achieve it. They are always wrong, of course, but even the worst of them are so convinced of democratic truths that they prefer to excuse their conduct on democratic grounds rather than assert that there is a higher ideal to which they owe allegiance.

Now all that is quite inconceivable to the great majority of Germans today. They just don't believe it. They have been reared on the directly opposing theories of racial superiority, supremacy of the state over the individual, glory of war, the natural duty of some to rule and many to obey, the absolute rightness of might.

Of course this is not because they are of German blood. As a matter of fact, Germans have made great contributions to democracy—but not in Germany. For many generations, Germany has been the world's greatest exporter of brains and character. That is why men like Carl Schurz and Wendell Willkie and Robert Wagner were making great additions to democratic processes in the United States instead of in the country of their ancestors.

There are German believers in democracy who probably would be willing to return to that country and attempt to bring the whole nation over to their way of thinking. There were even Germans inside Germany once who could have helped. They fought for human freedom, dignity and equality, and they died for their ideals with a courage which compelled the admiration of the world. But there never was a time in recent history when these democrats could sway the mass of the German people. So far as Germany herself is concerned, they have accomplished virtually nothing in the last seventy-five years. At every decisive moment, the "good" Germans have been neutralized or eliminated. In 1914, they joined the rest of their people in a war which nearly all of them approved. In 1919 they became a screen behind which the real Germany could lick its wounds and prepare for another war. In 1933, they were condemned to exile, the concentration camp or the headsman's block.

The optimistic belief that thousands of true German democrats survived the Nazi terror in exile or in underground movements rests upon no evidence so far as the German underground is concerned. The Nazis ruthlessly rooted out all opposition, and for years we heard little of the underground. When Allied troops took over Germany, the reason was apparent. The German underground had perished in Buchenwald and Dachau, its last representatives shipped home to relatives in those horrible little clay pots which Nazi brutality used as a final device of torture for the living.

A democratic form of government would have to be set up by outsiders, whether Germans in exile or Allies, and would be sustained either by Allied force or the belief of the German people that by submitting to democracy they could ease the terms to be granted them. This last was what happened after 1918. The Social Democrats accepted the blessing of the general staff to form a government. They adopted at Weimar a constitution which, on paper, was more democratic than our own. Certainly it undertook to guarantee all the freedoms of our own, and seemed to be as well protected with provisions for popular rule as any document could be. The supposedly democratic parties won overwhelming majorities in the earliest elections.

If such a regime could not break with the military past,

certainly there is nothing that could do so now. The Weimar Republic was not strong enough to take control of the Army out of the hands of its enemies. It dared not, or at least did not remove anti-republican judges, teachers and civil servants from their public duties, even when these functionaries openly agitated against democracy and the republic. On rare occasions when this grew too violent, or seemed to the timid men of Weimar to be compromising them in the eyes of the Allies, an official would be retired on a full pension, presumably to give him more time and scope for his political activities.

If a clash occurred between monarchists and republicans, Nazis and pacifists, the republicans and the pacifists took the more severe punishment. Men who exposed the illegal activities of the Army were murdered with impunity and some of these murders were rewarded later with high positions in the Nazi hierarchy. By 1930, the republic had lost so much of its peaceful disguise that the film "All Quiet on the Western Front," a pacifist picture based on one of the most popular of German books, was banned in Berlin.

As the German people rushed headlong down the road to war in the thirties, it was obvious that their experience under the republic had not converted any substantial proportion of them to democratic principles. On November 6, 1932, one of the many Reichstag dissolutions and elections that were employed in this period, apparently for the sole purpose of discrediting popular government, returned 196 Nazi deputies to a house of 584. Lacking a majority, the Nazis were not called upon to form a government; but no one else could, and on January 30, 1933,

Hitler moved into the Chancellery where a little less than ten years before General von Seeckt, with a single sentence, had turned thumbs down on his pretensions. The next day the Reichstag was dissolved again and new elections set for March 5.

Before that date, the German people had ample evidence that the Austrian corporal really had meant all the horrible things he had been shouting at them for years. Within five days of his accession to power, freedom of press and of assembly had been forbidden. By the end of February every right guaranteed under the Weimar constitution, which was still theoretically the law of the land, had been abrogated. A reign of terror swept the country. The Reichstag was burned, and plenty of people knew that the Nazis were the arsonists. Foes of the regime were beaten; Communists jailed; anti-Nazi meetings broken up.

Now a people who have faith in their own sovereignty do not tolerate this sort of thing. It is an unpardonably cynical view of humanity which can argue that any nation, even Germans, could be so intimidated by a gang of thugs that they would meekly vote by the tens of millions against their honest convictions. In the past just such tactics of terror in our own communities brought about the downfall of the Tweeds in American cities. But March 5, 1933, saw a very different response on the part of Germany's electorate. A smashing vote of confidence for intolerance, terror and dictatorship was given at the polls. The Nazis added ninety-two new seats to their Reichstag representation, and could boast with truth that they were the real spokesmen of the people. No party in the history of the republic had ever returned such a large block of deputies to the parliament.

The United Nations will be perpetrating a grim disservice to the cause of democracy if they impose a democratic form of government upon Germany. For it can be only form, not substance. The present generation have become the most fanatical haters of democracy ever known in the world. They have been taught with every artful device which a ruthless propaganda machine could invent that democratic regimes are weak, inefficient and corrupt. No government practicing the slightest degree of tolerance and freedom could possibly have operated so thorough a propaganda.

Furthermore, no government of practicing democrats, however efficient and idealistic, will be able to bring anything but suffering to the German people in the next few years. Every family will be mourning its dead and its cripples. Food shortages are and will continue to be extremely severe, the more so if the Germans are not encouraged by every means, and especially the destruction of their heavy industry, to grow their own crops on their own land. There is an acute housing problem and very little warm clothing. Medicines are bound to be scarce, and disease will be aggravated by hunger and cold.

The amount of relief that the United Nations can bring to Germany is bound to be inadequate. A dozen other countries in Europe are as greatly in need as the Germans and far more deserving. The United Nations have been able to spare shipping for only a minimum of relief needs for liberated areas. Peoples who bore the brunt of Nazi brutality should certainly have priority over a people who encouraged and supported and even shared that brutality.

Germans are human beings. Like all human beings, they will blame their sufferings on the government. For the Allies to saddle democracy with the odium of inevitable hardships will mean the destruction of any hope that a new generation of Germans might learn to understand and to embrace liberty.

If the new German government adopts a conciliatory or a fawning attitude toward the victors, it will earn the contempt of the German people. If it seeks to oppose Allied terms and defeat the conditions under which it is proposed to hold Germany in leash, it will earn the enmity of the United Nations. If it is a democratic regime, it will lose the support of the people in the first case and forfeit the support of the Allies in the second. Either way, democracy will be discredited.

The greatest mistake of those who urge a democratic form of government upon a reluctant German people is that they fail to grasp the realities of their subject. Democracy is one of those priceless things that cannot be given to anyone. It must be taken; it must be worked for; it must be earned. The real way to help democratic Germans to play a worth-while part in the development of freedom in their country is not to saddle them with the impossible job of governing a beaten, bitter nation. The real way is to give them the opportunity to be heard without the responsibility for the hardships that must come.

All this does not mean that the new government of Germany must be one of Nazis or Nazi sympathizers or militarists. But it should be recognized that there can be no possible German government which we could admire. We do not have to embrace our enemies; on the other hand, we do not have to impose the status of Quisling and Laval upon our friends, the German democrats in exile.

Germany herself offers a precedent which might be adapted to provide a government under which the country could be kept from repeating its excesses. In fact, the proposed regime might make it easier for the people to learn the real meaning of democracy. During the 1920's, there were several occasions when the complicated state of the parties made it impossible to form a Cabinet of party leaders. Sometimes new elections had to be called. Sometimes negotiations between the parties were unduly protracted.

In order to carry on the normal functions of government, therefore, the Germans resorted to the device of what was described as a ministry of civil servants—they called it a *Beamtenkabinett*. The members were supposed to be mostly officials in executive departments of the government. The chancellor was not a member of the Reichstag. If a deputy or party leader was included, he served theoretically as an individual, not as a representative of his political group. Some of these "civil servant governments" held office for quite some time. They had to make policy decisions and administrative decisions like any other Cabinet. Furthermore, they seem to have been at least up to the standard of the average German regime of the Weimar Republic.

Such a precedent might provide a reasonably sound German government for the immediate future. Once the civil service is purged of its most rabid Nazi fanatics, its war criminals and its violent supporters of militarist creeds, it would offer perhaps the most satisfactory instrument for carrying out the terms of peace. It will not be dependent upon the shifting party support of a maze of intriguing leaders. It will not expect to be popular. It will have the experience of administration. If we do not make the mistake of trusting it, it will serve to carry out the directions of Allied control commissions quite satisfactorily.

Sentimentalists to whom the memory of German music and beer festivals is stronger than the memory of Lidice and Maidaneck will shake their heads at this program. They have a great faith in the essential goodness of people. But unfortunately it is a faith like that which launched the Children's Crusade of the Middle Ages. For the sake of humanity and for the sake of the very ideals which these sentimentalists wish Germany to develop, we cannot afford to attempt to defeat the armed might of the infidel with only the weapons of innocence and ignorance, hope and charity, sweetness and light.

Chapter XI

PEACE SCHOOL FOR GERMANS

IN DISCUSSIONS OF WHAT TO DO WITH Germany, she has been compared to a mental patient, a problem child, a whole zoo of animals ranging from snakes to apes, a case of retarded development, a young girl led astray, a slab of molten metal ready for the molder and much else besides. Such similes have merit, chiefly as emphasizing the educational or evolutionary problem that must be faced before the German people can be considered no longer a menace to peace.

A great many individuals are burning with a laudable zeal to undertake the great reform. It is a task worthy of the highest, most selfless missionary spirit. To redeem this virile, capable people from their worship of force and their lust for war would obviously be one of the noblest services that could be performed for mankind. It is a service which will require that the devoted teachers and preachers of the gospel of peace be supported by the nations who are already believers.

But it must achieve a real conversion. It will not be enough that the old Teuton gods of war and destruction be renamed for the saints of peace, while the old rites of human sacrifice are continued in the old way under new forms. That has happened before. This time we must be sure that the Germans do more than understand what we are talking about when we speak of the sanctity of life, the rights and duties of individuals, the equality of men and the place of the state as a servant of its citizens. In the past these phrases were entirely without meaning for most Germans. The world will be quite safe from these people only when they not only grasp the meaning but believe in the truth of what they have learned.

There are two completely wrong approaches to this great experiment in pedagogy. One is the approach of the fond parent who cannot bear to see a child's tears, so overlooks the worst behavior with a kindly: "There now, don't do it again." The other is the approach of the enraged parent who thinks evil can be exorcised if the arm that wields the whip is tireless enough. Of course Germany is not a child, but she would respond no better to either of these courses of treatment.

The re-education of Germany needs to be approached in a scientific spirit before it is safe to allow missionary fervor free rein. Judging by the facts of history, along with what we know of human nature in general and German nature in particular, certain fundamental procedures seem obvious.

First of all, Germany must be disarmed in her own mind as well as in reality. The most fertile soil for the seed of democracy would be those Germans who know it is useless to plot for dictatorships, war and conquest. There is no point in a dictatorship unless it be for war, and no incentive for Germans to fight unless they think they can win. The elementary lesson for the German people is that there is no use planning and working for war because they will not have the means to wage it.

The only possible way to make that lesson effective is to make it true. As long as Germany has her heavy industries, it will not be true. For then there will always be the possibility of renewing the battle. Always in the back of millions of German minds will be the thought that, although the Reich failed twice to achieve first place in the world by force of arms, the third time she might prove luckier.

Deprived of blast furnaces, synthetics factories, machine tool and heavy machinery plants, gigantic power installations, Germans will have more reason to think of peace. In time they might come to appreciate its blessings. Even in their fanaticism, Germans as a whole retain a certain practical sense. Only a relatively harmless minority could go on year after year conspiring for conquest in a vacuum, knowing that the means of conquest were entirely out of reach. When the majority of the German people are small farmers, they will be a bit less susceptible to the lure of militarism. The owners of land, especially the owners who actually work it themselves, are likely to have little time for other occupations and to be impatient of military service which calls their sons from home at harvest time. The peasants of Germany as a class took the Nazi virus later and in somewhat milder form than many of their fellow citizens.

Of course destruction of German heavy industry will not automatically turn the German people into paths of peace. The existence of heavy industry, however, will serve as an insurmountable barrier to getting them started along those paths. Once the road is clear, the constructive educational process can begin.

It will be argued that the Germans will not like it, that they will be exasperated and revengeful, brooding over their wrongs and quite untamable. Of course, it is not essential that the Germans like the program for their future. Actually they are not going to like most of the fate that is bound to overtake them. But, they will be far less likely to harbor dreams of vengeance if they have a plain course of rehabilitation open to them. Such a course is the reclaiming of their own soil and the working of their own consumer goods industries, which can be a faster and more certain road out of postwar confusion than any other.

When the possibilities for new aggression have been removed, the big educational task can begin. It cannot, however, be done by anyone except the Germans themselves. There is no record in history of any civilized people permitting themselves to be educated in a whole new way of life by foreign masters. Even barbarous nations have been destroyed or left in barbarism more often than they have adopted the culture of their conquerors. Thus Spain was able to eliminate the Aztec and Inca civilizations but not impose her own to any marked extent. The Germans themselves have failed utterly to Nazify the minorities within their own borders or to "re-educate" France, Holland, Belgium, Norway, Poland and the rest in a German manner.

The education we should propose might seem much more attractive than anything the Germans have to offer, so it might be supposed that it would "take" more readily. The only difficulty on that score is that, in their present stage of development, our education is not more attractive to Germans. They have been quite thoroughly exposed to democratic ideas in the past, at least through the medium of books and plays and movies, lectures and debates, most of the normal educational processes. Germans were great students of foreign languages, literature and history. Their learned men were frequently observed to know more about other countries, including our own, than the citizens of those countries. The works of outstanding British and American authors were best sellers in Germany for many years. But not for long enough. The supposedly high standards of German scholarship cracked, with genuine relief to the scholars, when the Nazis staged their elaborate book burnings, consigning the classics of Western democracy to flames which alone have never yet destroyed an idea. But the democratic idea was distasteful, often incomprehensible to many of the most cultivated Germans. Sigrid Undset, the distinguished Norwegian author, noted this phenomenon and wrote:

> I have talked with German scientists and writers who defended the book-burnings and frankly told about their emotions during the ceremony. "—After all these things were not in harmony with our true nature, and we were grateful to be permitted at long last to stop admiring alien cultures and be ourselves." The young scholar who said this was in many ways an attractive, kind and sensitive man who had done good work in his own field of philology.

The long, slow process of eradicating this spirit from Germany cannot begin too soon. Undoubtedly a few precautionary steps besides the elimination of heavy industry will have to be taken first. German schools and universities should certainly have their textbooks cleaned of the medieval dogma of their last dozen years. Nazis and Nazi sympathizers should be removed from the faculties. Newspapers and other periodicals, radio broadcasts, theaters should be put under controls which will insure an end to preachings of the Nazi creed.

Then we can come back to the constructive measures. And only then will we learn the truth of the claim that a great many Germans are eager or at least willing to absorb the principles of democracy. The exiles will return—some of them—with enthusiasm for their evangelical task. Probably it will prove heartbreakingly slow. In his study of Teutonic paranoia, *Is Germany Incurable?*, Dr. Richard Brickner presumed the existence of "a sizable number of individuals, however unorganized and unaware of one another," who are free from the German war madness. We can hope that he is right, and that such individuals may become the nucleus for a regenerated Reich.

Against them—and against the returning exiles and against whatever influences the United Nations may throw in—will be an overwhelming mass resistance to new ideas. Stemming from the most powerful educational force of all, the family, this resistance will be exceedingly difficult to crack. It is the bitter fruit of years of far more intensive cultivation than we will be able to afford for a long time to come. Even if it were possible to control completely what is taught in schools, what is said on the radio, what is printed in periodicals, the family influence can outweigh all of them. There used to be a theory that a child's thinking was conditioned by the time it was seven, and such conditioning is done almost entirely in the family. Millions of Germans have been raised as fanatic Nazis. Most of the men and women who are and will become parents have been pretty thoroughly debased and brutalized by Nazi education. The potential fathers of Germany, the returning soldiers, have participated in atrocities, helped to loot foreign peoples and will remember with nostalgia the days of their supremacy. That longing for a return of the day of the oppressor will be communicated to their children in the stories of old soldiers looking back fondly to the adventurous period when they could consider themselves and very nearly were the masters of Europe.

Before that deep educational force can be overcome, a whole new generation of parents must be born and raised in an entirely different atmosphere. Meanwhile, their redemption can take place only if the means for war have been taken so far away from the new generation that conquest and battles are not to be thought of seriously.

The theory that gentle kindness can take the place of this essential is based on an unconscious acceptance of one of the cleverest points of German propaganda between the two wars. This was the never-ending plaint that the Germans had been unfairly humiliated in the peace of 1919, that they were oppressed by the victors, that their better instincts were crushed by poverty and betrayal. A short and simple answer was given by that queer, typically German genius, Oswald Spengler, author of *The Decline of the West*, when he said:

"The legend that a mild peace could have prevented a second World War could only have originated in the heads that have never studied the German mind."

Actually the Versailles terms were as mild as they could have been made. The theory that the German people would respond to moderation was held by most of the leading spirits in the Paris peace conference. Yet the Germans complained. They found the territorial settlements unfair. Who now proposes to let them keep Alsace and Lorraine or the Polish Corridor? The Germans resented their loss of colonies. Who proposes to give them any now, in the light of their record as rulers over other peoples? The Germans protested that the reparations exacted were too high. Well, they never paid them. They resented the presence of foreign troops on their soil. Does anyone think we will not need an occupying force this time or that it should be removed five years ahead of schedule? Germans cried out against the treaty clause by which they acknowledged guilt for the war. Would anyone propose that we acquit them of the guilt for this war?

The history of recent years is an even better answer than Spengler's to the notion that mildness will bring out hidden good traits in the German people. The Germans for most of the period between the two world wars enjoyed a higher standard of living than the majority of their neighbors. They had enough left over to build the mightiest war machine the world had ever known up to that time. And they became progressively more bitter foes of decency and peace.

At one time, too, it was the fashion to blame Nazism and the rise of Hitler on the great depression. Now that tragedy was not a purely German event. It was worldwide, and Germany suffered no more than most of the other countries in the same period. Unemployment was relatively little greater in the Reich than in the United States in 1932. Some statisticians compute it as even less. The depths had been reached by both countries in late 1932. It was in the American tradition to look for a leader who could help them out of their troubles through the democratic processes we are used to. The election of Franklin D. Roosevelt was the result. Just twelve weeks later the German people acted quite as strictly in accord with their traditions. They turned to a dictator to lead them out of their troubles through war. Hitler as Chancellor was the result of this.

The consensus of opinion of those who know Germany best is that the people have been so elaborately trained in obedience that they are genuinely uncomfortable unless unquestioned authority is giving them orders. To Americans, one of whose greatest joys is telling off the government, it is strange that the average German would no more think of questioning the wisdom and rightness of his rulers than he would think of objecting to military service.

Most of the sincere German exceptions are in exile or in their graves. It is to the survivors, of course, that we must look for the beginnings of a new German civilization based on peace. But we would be doing them no favor to encourage any notion that this is the work of a single generation or less. The actual physical facts of schooling show up the impossibility. The German educational system in prewar days needed more than a quarter of a million teachers to staff it. Those teachers have been indoctrinated with Nazi philosophy; most of them did not need to go very far to embrace it, for they were the product of Fichte and Nietzsche and von Treitschke.

If there were other teachers in Germany, they too are in exile or dead. For the time being there are not nearly enough German teachers to staff the schools with sincere democrats. Even if it would be effective to use foreign teachers, it would be impossible to find them in sufficient quantities. All the United Nations have arrears of education in their own countries to catch up with. The United States would probably be in as good a position to furnish the men and women for this task as any. Yet our own educators have been complaining of the shortage of teachers for our own schools.

Without offering exceptionally high wages and other inducements, it would be impossible to recruit volunteers for the job in Germany. Even to mention drafting American teachers for service in the Reich is to expose the folly of such a suggestion. But there would be well-founded and very loud outcries from our own people if we embarked upon a policy of luring teachers needed in our own schools to send them overseas for the doubtful experiment of converting the German people to love of democracy.

The most any occupying authority can reasonably hope to do is to prevent the worst excesses of the old German education from being repeated openly. We can exercise supervision over textbooks, films and other teaching aids. That should be done, too, by highly qualified personnel who will not permit their efforts to degenerate into an empty routine which would be easy to evade and which would concern itself rather with the letter than the spirit.

For the rest, experience must become the great German teacher. The elementary schools, for example, will probably be staffed for years by the sort of pedagogue who survived if he did not actually participate in the German orgy of organized miseducation. Traces of the old teachings will crop up from time to time, for they will be a persistent undercurrent in all German scholastic thought.

The current can dry up only after a period of many years, and only if it is not fed by fresh streams. Better than any board of censorship or commissioner of education in preventing renewed propaganda for German militarism would be the elimination of the heavy industrialist and the Junker—the first by destruction of his factories, the second by breaking up his estates. These two groups will then be powerless to finance the sort of education to which they have contributed wealth and influence in the past. They will not be able to subsidize newspapers and books, lecturers and films.

But let us not delude ourselves that this of itself will regenerate Germany's educational system. For many years to come, her schools and colleges will be nothing but a disappointment to believers in freedom. Such believers will be strongly tempted to attempt a revolution in German education. They can try, but they should not be too upset if they achieve little progress. They will cry out against the iniquity of allowing such and such heresies to be taught in German schools. They will perform a valuable service, too, in keeping our attention on the German problem. But they will not solve that problem. So far as education is concerned, the Germans will have to do most of that themselves.

Chapter XII

DIVIDE AND CONQUER

TWO GERMANYS WOULD BE EASIER TO deal with than one. The anxieties of other nations would be considerably relieved if the Reich could be split, because in the odd arithmetic of international politics it is not true that two halves are equal to the whole. They are substantially less, and if the halves are German, the threat to peace is diminished by just that amount.

No matter how much two national administrations are agreed, no matter how friendly their peoples, they cannot act as quickly or as forcefully as if the same resources were under one government. It is the old story of a single nation being a match for a coalition of greater potential strength. The United Nations during the war brought coalition enterprise to new heights of efficiency. They did it largely by putting all their troops under a single commander in each theater of war. But the men whose energy and tact have made this possible would be the first to admit that, despite general and close agreement, some inconvenience is caused by the minor delays needed for consultation, by the compromises required to adjust slight differences of policy and by the looser organization inevitable when there can be no single fount of final authority. Therefore, a divided Germany would be weaker than a united country, even though the division is essentially artificial.

Partition has a rather ugly sound to free men. It recalls the various dismemberments of Poland by predatory nations. It recalls the ruthless way in which European powers split up most of Africa among themselves with little regard to the inhabitants. It smacks of all too many past ventures in creating spheres of influence.

Actually, the partition of Germany would have nothing in common with these examples of a discredited imperialism. There is no intention of making the two separate segments of the German state a part of an alien community, nor of parceling them out under the overlordship of different masters. Each of the two would have as much independence and freedom as the single Germany could be permitted, perhaps more since they would not be so dangerous.

The real question about partition is whether it would work. Like all the other proposed "solutions" of the German problem, it would not be enough in itself to end the danger of aggression. And, like so many of the measures which will be necessary, partition could be effective only so far as it contributed to barring Germany from the means to renew her wars of conquest. It would be quite useless unless heavy industry were forbidden both parts of the dismembered Reich.

Heavy industry would make a sham out of any division. In the past, the strength of the big industrialists and the hidden general staff constituted the real government of Germany. If they were to be allowed to exist, it would make very little difference to the rest of the world what sort of government and how many the country enjoyed. The rest of the world would be under the constant threat of aggression from the same groups which have twice plunged the world into war. Heavy industry would provide the central authority which partition would seek to break. The same combine that controls the steel of the Ruhr and the chemical plants of Westphalia would dominate a government in Berlin and another in Munich quite as easily as it could operate a couple of branch offices. It is sound logic for those who object to the elimination of heavy industry to protest against partition, too. The German militarists themselves would accept partition with much better grace than the destruction of their real sources of power.

But, granted the destruction of German heavy industry, a "slight dismemberment" of the Reich could help achieve the eventual goal of reclaiming Germany for the society of nations. It would be a charitable application of the Nazi technique of divide and conquer. We would be dividing a nation physically, not spiritually, and conquering its belligerent habits.

It is sometimes argued that if partition of Germany into two parts is a good thing, three would be better and thirty better still. Sumner Welles, in *The Time for Decision*, advocates breaking up Germany into three parts. He would form a southern German state comprising the predominantly Catholic areas of Bavaria, Wuerttemberg, Baden, Hesse-Darmstadt, the Rhineland and the Saar; a northwestern state consisting mainly of Upper Hesse, Thuringia, Westphalia, Hanover, Oldenburg and Hamburg; a northeastern state composed of Prussia (minus East Prussia, which would go to Poland), Mecklenburg and Saxony. The plan would enable each section to achieve economic security. Other advocates of partition have urged the breaking up of the Reich into the many component parts of pre-Bismarckian days.

However, there is a *reductio ad absurdum* even in dealing with Germany. The Allied aim should be the weakening of Germany to a point where she ceases to be a danger to the world, not a series of divisions that would lead to confusion which in itself could become perilous. The partition into two states rather than the three of Welles is recommended here chiefly because it is proposed to internationalize the Ruhr, which would be an integral part of one of his German nation's. Several other territorial adjustments suggested by Welles would leave a somewhat larger Germany than would be contained in the two part division—such as parts of the old Polish Corridor and Schleswig, which Welles would leave to Germany. Under the alternative two-state arrangement, the prewar Germany should suffer four major territorial losses as follows:

1. East Prussia and southern Silesia, which would be incorporated into Poland.
2. The Saar basin and its adjacent territories bounded by the Rhine and Moselle rivers, which would be ceded to France.
3. The territory between the Danish border and the Kiel Canal, which would be ceded to Denmark.
4. Parts of the Rhineland, which would be ceded to Belgium and the Netherlands if they desired it.

Out of the remains of the old German Reich would be formed a South German State consisting of Bavaria, Wuerttemberg, Baden and certain adjacent territories, joined with an independent Austria by a customs union;

a North German state comprising a large part of the old Prussia, Saxony, Thuringia and several smaller states.

The cession of the Saar region to France will strengthen that country both strategically and industrially. The French steel mills, which for many years had to depend upon German coal supplies very largely, would be independent. The French would thus receive some compensation for the damage done them.

The transfer of East Prussia and southern Silesia to Poland would eliminate that geographical and political monstrosity, the Polish Corridor. It would give Poland access to the Baltic as the Treaty of Versailles intended twenty-five years ago but in a less involved and controversial manner. It would remove the greatest of the Junker estates and the cradle of Junkerdom itself from the Reich. It would give Poland the coal and the industries with which to develop a better balanced economy than she was able to build between the two wars. It would, in short, be the creation of that "strong and independent Poland" which was one of the Allied war aims.

The grants of territory to Denmark, Belgium and the Netherlands are chiefly designed to compensate them for losses suffered during the German occupation. The Netherlands are entitled to lands to replace those flooded and ruined by the Germans in their retreat. The area for Denmark is largely Danish in population, and its removal from Germany would make international control of the Kiel Canal a little easier.

In all these territorial adjustments, the old-fashioned practice of handing over large groups of people to a government they do not like and a foreign one at that should be avoided. It is no longer necessary to be bound by the old feudal conception that the people go with the land. Germans in ceded territories can be transferred to the new German states; minority groups left within the German borders will be given every opportunity to move to the country of their racial kinsmen if they desire to do so.

The postwar period will be a good one in which to carry out such shifts of population. A great many people will be homeless, and particularly in the districts which are to change hands. A great many people will have to be repatriated, most of them because they were dragged from their homes by Germany to work for her, some because they fled the rising tide of war. To this mass movement of people must be added as a minimum the return to the Reich of all Germans from those areas, including internationally controlled land, which will no longer be part of the two German states. The opportunity for propaganda would be too tempting if they were left behind. The Nazis taught us that. All their prewar aggressions were preceded by a wave of hysterical anguish about imagined ill-treatment of the noble German minorities of Czechoslovakia or Poland or Memel as the case might be.

There have been ample modern precedents for such hegiras. Some of them have been extremely beneficial to all the peoples concerned. The largest was the exchange of populations between Greece and Turkey after the war of 1922. More than a million individuals were moved from one side of the border to the other, and both Greece and Turkey have testified that the move was an important factor in the development of their now friendly rela-

PROPOSAL FOR POST-WAR GERMAN BOUNDARIES

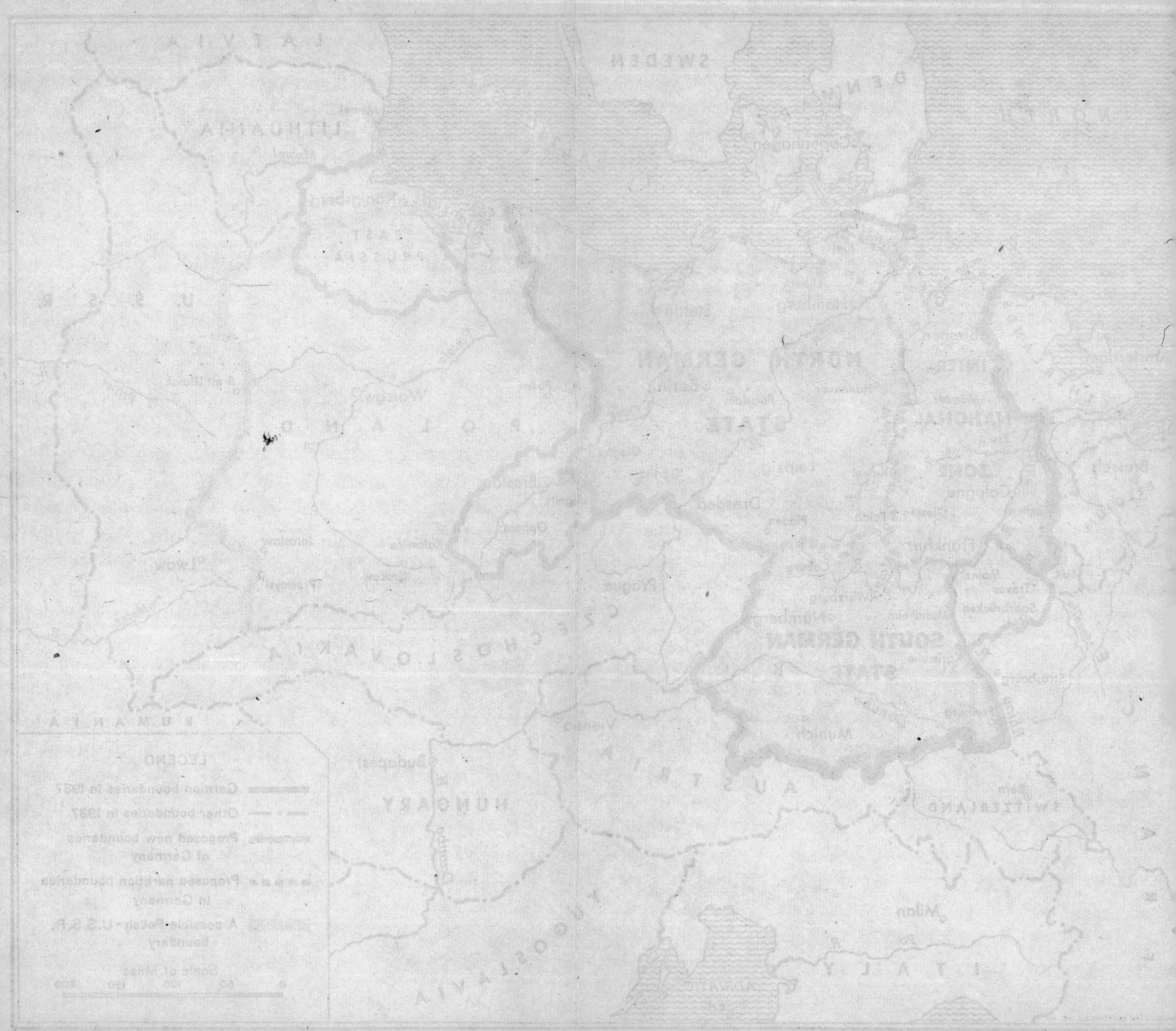

tions. Germany and Italy carried out a minor exchange to end Tyrolean nationalism, and Germany also brought back to the Reich many thousands of Baltic Germans.

Partition and repatriation will be aided in achieving their purpose by decentralization. State governments might be set up not only in the eighteen pre-Hitler German states but each of the provinces of Prussia. If given a large degree of local autonomy, these state governments could further weaken the potential power of Germany for aggression without causing any additional suffering within Germany.

The main danger of partition and decentralization is that they would be regarded as sufficient in themselves, or with a few other precautionary measures, to insure German behavior. It is argued that the principal motivating force of German militarism has been Prussia and the Prussian-modeled general staff, so that danger of militarism will be avoided by splitting off and isolating Prussia. Historical, cultural, religious and economic differences are cited as evidence that the dismembered German states would not want to reunite.

The United Nations can fall into a trap if they rely upon any such pleasant theories to solve the German problem for them. It is true that Prussia was the mainspring of German belligerence and that national unity was necessary and will be necessary to prosecute a successful war. But it is by no means proved that partition would end the danger; on the contrary, it is possible to demonstrate just the opposite. The German states attacked France in 1870 before their unification; in fact, unification was the result of the victory.

Since then, Prussian militarism has become German militarism. It is only necessary to look over the roster of Nazi leaders to see how widely the Prussian infection has spread. Hitler was an Austrian; Himmler and Goering, Bavarians; Alfred Rosenberg, a Balt; Hjalmar Schacht, from Schleswig; Otto Meissner, a German Alsatian; von Neurath, a Wuerttemberger. Even during World War I there was some sectionalism apparent in the Army. Troops fought as Bavarians, Saxons and so on. In World War II there were no such divisions. Prisoners certainly have not shown any feeling of having been oppressed by Prussia; in fact the old state names have disappeared from their conversation. They are proud to call themselves Germans; they may call themselves storm troopers or elite guards or airmen, but they put little emphasis on being Thuringians or Hessians.

The German opposition to unification, which existed to some extent in 1870, has completely disappeared since then. And even at that time Pan-Germanism was a far stronger force than German separatism. The intensive propaganda about the master race went on under Bismarck, under Kaiser Wilhelm, under the Weimar Republic and with fanatical intensity under Hitler. Separation would hardly overcome the national feeling, and would prove a very weak barrier against German aggression if it stood alone. It will have to be established from outside; it could be maintained only by outside force in the long run, and it is more than likely that as the years go on, the Allies would not be willing to use their armies indefinitely to keep the various segments of the German people from reuniting.

The scheme of partition and decentralization, then, can be considered only as an advanced outpost in the world's defenses of its security. Like all such advanced outposts, it can easily be overwhelmed by a determined enemy. Unless there are much stronger inner defenses, the fortress—in this case world peace—is doomed. The strongest bastion is the elimination of heavy industries. Actually, if heavy industries remain, there will be an enemy within the fortress itself. For the German magnates will have complete control over the outposts. When we remember how powerfully the German cartels influenced Allied manufacturers and even Allied governments, we get a faint idea of how completely they could dominate a couple of governments of their own puppets.

Probably the greatest service that partition and decentralization can make to the cause of peace is that they will serve the purpose of any well planned outpost. That is to guard against surprise, to delay the attackers and to be sacrificed in the moment of crisis. Partition could put the rest of the world on its guard; when the separate German states join together again, it will be a warning that we should watch for other signs of possible aggression. Partition can delay and hamper any future German plans for an attack upon other countries. But in case of another war, we could expect to see German state lines vanish without a trace.

Chapter XIII

DISARMAMENT AND CONTROLS

THE BEST PAPER PROGRAM HUMAN wisdom could devise for dealing with Germany will be worse than useless unless it is put into operation and kept in operation. The most terrible menace to peace ever loosed upon the earth is fresh enough in our memories so that Allied governments and Allied peoples now understand that only their own unity saved them.

The life expectancy of that understanding is the life expectancy of peace. It will be measured, almost in actuarial terms, by the Allied program for dealing with Germany. But practical measures to prevent a new upsurge of the Teutonic fury can last only as long as the will to enforce them animates all of the great coalition for peace which has been called into being by Axis aggression.

It will not be enough to have these sentiments kept bright and burning only in Germany's nearest neighbors. Apathy among those a little further removed from immediate peril (although in modern war that can only be a very little) will give a new set of German warmongers their chance to squirm out from the restrictions which bind them over to keep the peace. By playing on the sympathy, the indecision and the indifference of the forgetful nations, Germans will be able to block the efforts of those who remember. The countries which wish to keep the German threat from developing will be chided as harboring belligerent attitudes. The essential quality of unity will be lost. Any program for disarming Germany and keeping her disarmed will go overboard with Allied solidarity.

We do not have to theorize about this any more than we would about the probable effect of dropping a bottle of milk on the pavement. We have seen with our own eyes that the bottle will break and the milk will spill. We have also seen with our own eyes the breaking of a high international determination to prevent any resurgence of German military power. First on the list of Allied war aims in 1917, it hardly survived the interval between the Armistice and the Peace Conference.

Victory brought so many problems that seemed to strike closer home than the future of a beaten Germany! And anyway, we'd won, hadn't we? So a large part of the world turned its back on the real purpose of the great crusade. It became almost a fashion to sneer at both the fears and the hopes which had inspired the Allies. But there were other influences than indifference at work sapping the will of the Allies to prevent German aggression from breaking out again.

There was the terrible war weariness which rebelled at every new effort. There was the confused, generous, foolish sentiment which regarded war as a game and argued that the sporting gesture was to help pick up an adversary after you had knocked him down. There was the disillusionment which took the form of isolationism in the hope that if we kept our eyes averted the rest of the world would go away. There was the shortsighted grab for the fleeting profit. Some businessmen and some governments were tempted by the prospect of a big German market to urge the Allies to let the beaten nation build up its industry without interference. They soon lost the German market in the Reich's economic war of the thirties and a good deal of their trade in the rest of the world too.

The weakening of the world's will to peace was the fundamental factor in the rearmament of Germany. From that all the others stemmed. But the contributing causes for the failure of the plan established in the Versailles Treaty were many and formidable. Some of them can be traced to the earliest cracks in the determination to keep Germany disarmed, cracks which appeared almost as soon as victory was won. Others were due to an understandable underestimate of the problem. It is largely because the Versailles settlement failed so signally that we can obtain the benefit of hindsight in these matters. There was an excuse for the negotiators at Paris for they were venturing into new territory and did not recognize the new phenomena. There can be no excuse for us if we repeat their mistakes.

The Versailles Treaty was long on undertakings for Germany but short on methods of enforcing them or of informing the Allied governments as to the progress of German compliance. The chief guarantee for the execution of the treaty's terms was the occupation of the Rhineland. This territory was divided into three zones one to be evacuated in five, the next in ten, and the last in fifteen years if the treaty was observed. Violations of the treaty could lead to longer occupation. The march of French and

Belgian troops into the Ruhr in 1923 was an attempt to enforce reparations payments.

There was also an Inter-Allied Control Commission to supervise German disarmament. It had a great many more powers in the treaty than it was ever able to exercise in Germany. One reason for this was the fact that except in the case of reparations, where specific sanctions were proposed for German violations, the treaty relied for enforcement upon two attractive but frail theories. One was a curious faith that there would exist in Germany a genuine good will toward living up to the treaty obligations she assumed under duress. The other was a belief that the League of Nations would be able to deal with infractions in a judicial but firm spirit.

The basis of the first fallacy was the very unsoldierly appearance of the predominantly Social Democratic German government of that day and the apparent humility of the German people. The second was doomed to failure, as any international organization now would be, by the failure of the United States to take part and by the immediate and fundamental split between the two chief remaining Allies, France and England, on policies to be pursued. England was speedily converted from her "Hang-the-Kaiser" mood of 1918 to a belief that the German tiger had become a kitten to be tamed by kindness. Between these two, the German question never was referred to the League at all, although Article 213 of the Versailles Treaty reads:

"So long as the present Treaty remains in force, Germany undertakes to give every facility for any investigation which the Council of the League of Nations, acting if need be by a majority vote, may consider necessary."

This was one of the few circumstances in which the Council could act without unanimity. It was never invoked because there never was a time when a majority was really in earnest about nipping the German armaments menace.

The reliance on German good will in disarmament matters was evidenced by the fact that after Germany was disarmed the control commissions were not to continue to see that she remained disarmed. The British and French had proposed and argued for such an extension. But Woodrow Wilson believed that if disarmament was to be effective, the world would have to follow Germany in this respect and that by then the League of Nations would be the medium for enforcing all international obligations.

The program of clipping German claws proceeded vigorously enough in the beginning. Three commissions were set up to direct military, naval and air disarmament. Germany was ordered to supply the commissions with all documents, blueprints and designs of a military value. The commissions and their inspectors were to have full freedom of movement through the country. Germany was to supply any labor or facilities these commissions needed for delivery or destruction of arms. Regional control commissions were set up in various parts of the country to make the supervision more thorough. Germany established her own military peace commission and liaison offices ostensibly to co-operate with the control bodies.

All that was missing was the German desire to co-operate and a sustained Allied will to see the job through. The personnel of the control commissions worked hard, but their own countries showed little interest and Germany opposed to their best efforts a universal passive resistance varied with positive acts of sabotage and evasion.

It proved impossible for the commissions to root out the secret caches of arms which were used to train the illegal military formations. Actually this was the only purpose served by the weapons left over from the war; the Germans knew quite well that their main job was to retain facilities for making new instruments of war which would render the old ones obsolete.

However, the inspection of German factories was the key to real disarmament. Here the Germans performed their most effective sabotage. Some seven thousand plants were theoretically under Allied supervision. The Germans insisted that representatives of the Allies should visit them only after giving previous notice and in company with a member of the local German liaison office set up to "co-operate" in disarmament. The reason given was that this procedure alone could protect the Allied agents from violence on the part of Germans whose sense of national honor might be outraged by the notion of living up to their pledged word. Another German regulation, which even its propounders could not excuse on altruistic grounds, provided that only certain leading officials in each factory might supply visiting representatives of the Allied commissions with information. This was designed to keep the inspectors from getting any real data from disgruntled or honest workmen, engineers or shipping clerks.

The result was that considerable quantities of arms were removed to remote, secret hideouts. Members of the Allied commissions were boycotted at hotels and restaurants, particularly in the smaller towns. Inspectors were attacked by hoodlums, and the German government brushed the incidents aside as the responsibility of municipal or state authorities.

The petty infringements were chiefly valuable to Germany in wearing out Allied enthusiasm for the job and concealing the real direction of German rearmament. This last would have been extremely difficult to detect by any system of inspection provided in the treaty. The real power of German militarism was being forged in the blast furnaces of the Ruhr, the chemical plants of Westphalia, the shipyards of Hamburg and Bremen, the electrical works of Silesia. Here were being produced articles which the negotiators of Versailles had never considered in terms of military power. But their use for war was being planned by the clandestine general staff, by the scientists in a hundred research laboratories and by experiments abroad, out of reach of Allied control. In that way, Germans were building experimental submarines in Spain; Krupp was testing new kinds of weapons in Russian factories built by German engineers; new and better guns were being built in the German-controlled Bofors works of Sweden; warlike experiments that could not be hidden in Germany were being carried out in Swiss laboratories. At home, the future Luftwaffe was getting its training in a booming German civil aviation. Then in 1926 the Allied commissions were withdrawn on the ground that Germany had been disarmed within the meaning of the treaty.

It was typical of the Allied control system that at no time was it able to cope with the many secret military groups which were drilling all over the country. Everyone knew they were in existence; the leaders of many of them could be pointed out by every foreign correspondent in Germany. Only after the departure of the commissions were these groups liquidated. Then it was done promptly and efficiently by the Reichswehr itself, which felt strong enough to carry on the work of new war preparations without the help of most of these illegal organizations.

The abolition of the relatively inefficient secret groups was easy for the general staff because they had served their purpose. In large measure, this was to keep alive the tradition of the officer class. The old family ties to the Army were so greatly intensified in this period of "disarmament" that by 1930 two-thirds of all the Weimar Republic's army officers were members of the traditional military families. The imperial army of 1913 had drawn only one-fourth of its officers from this class.

The Versailles Treaty's chief machinery for control of Germany turned out to be an unsuccessful collection agency. This was the Reparations Commission and the various, changing bodies set up to force Germany to pay. Significantly, it was only in the case of reparation defaults that the peace treaty provided specific sanctions. The provision actually read:

> The measures which the Allied and Associated Powers shall have the right to take, in case of voluntary default by Germany, and which Germany agrees not to regard as acts of war, may include economic and financial prohibitions and reprisals and in general such other measures as the respective governments may determine to be necessary in the circumstances.

In May, 1921, the Allies issued at London an ultimatum designed to collect reparations. Germany accepted it, and a Committee of Guarantees was appointed to see that it was carried out. Under this program, a special 25 per cent tax on all German exports was to be collected for reparations and all import duties were earmarked for the same purpose. But there was no provision by which the Allies could exercise any real authority over German appropriations, and the Committee of Guarantees had its headquarters in Paris instead of Berlin as the French had desired.

The collapse of this system led the French and Belgians into the Ruhr, and that adventure led in turn to the Dawes plan. The experts who drew it up in 1924 were convinced that reparations ought to be settled on a business rather than a political basis. They thought German credit would be damaged by the possibility of sanctions imposed for "voluntary default." Therefore, at the suggestion of the Dawes group, the Allies agreed to change this to "flagrant default." So far as it made any difference, it was a concession to Germany.

The new machinery for enforcement was designed to avoid interference as much as possible with German internal affairs. However, since new German revenues including a part of railway receipts, were assigned to the reparations account, there had to be some supervision. Several commissioners were appointed for this purpose, and foreigners were to serve on the boards of the railways and the Reichsbank. Over them all was an Agent General of Reparations in Berlin. But all these officials were permitted only to watch what went on. They had no control over the German budget, German taxation, German foreign trade or German expenditures. Even these watchers were abandoned with the Young plan in 1930.

The work of the Dawes Committee in putting the final quietus on attempts to enforce reparations provisions was helped by the opinion drawn up in London that same year by a group of Allied jurists. These experts pronounced with judicial authority and dignity that the Allies had no legal power to infringe on Germany's sovereign right to decide how she would produce the sums demanded as reparations. This opinion colored the whole subsequent treatment of the problem. It was a notable example of the flagging will to prevent another war.

The whole experience, so thoroughly unfortunate and disillusioning, can be of enormous value in appraising just how much can be accomplished with Germany through disarmament and controls this time. Recognizing the limitations of the method, it ought to be possible to fit them into a more complete machine for preventing another German military effort.

The actual confiscation of existing stocks of munitions is being pushed more vigorously this time. Opportunities for concealment are reduced because the occupation forces extend throughout the country instead of being confined to the Rhineland. But of course some weapons have been hidden. Not even the Nazis, using much more brutal methods than are being employed against the Germans, were able to disarm completely the determined resistance movements of occupied territory.

But no German General Staff would think of starting another war with the weapons of this one. New and much more terrible means of destruction would have to be worked out and put into production before the militarists would be ready to make the appeal to arms. Therefore, the task of the United Nations is to establish such controls over Germany as will prevent the growth of another arms industry. Profiting by the experience of our failures in the past and our all too well-founded suspicions of the future, this should involve five sets of controls. They should be aimed at:

1. Preventing the rise of any political movements in the military, Nazi or Pan-German tradition.
2. Preventing the same influences from creeping into German channels of information and education.
3. Preventing facilities for the production of armaments.
4. Preventing the transfer of a German nucleus for aggression to some other country where it could operate until a chance to repatriate it occurs, and suppressing those already established in countries that have been sympathetic to Nazism.
5. Preventing scientific and industrial research which could lead to development of new military techniques.

One set of controls which may seem rather obvious is omitted here, although it is a rather attractive theory built up out of the wartime experience of all the belligerent nations. It is increasingly plain to us that a thoroughgoing system of rationing, pricing, priorities, wage fixing, taxation and currency control can direct the energies of a nation in almost any desired direction. Therefore, at first glance, it would seem that if the Allies simply take over these functions and responsibilities in Germany, they can settle everything. It is a beautiful and alluring vision. It has only one drawback; it will not work.

We have seen that in the first few months of Allied occupation. The contrast between the controls set up to govern Germany's internal economy and those which concern her economic relations with the outside world has been striking. Although the German governmental agency which had supervised foreign exchange and foreign trade had virtually disappeared, leaving almost no records, the Army's and the Treasury's program for foreign exchange and blocking were being well executed within a matter of weeks. Very sensibly, officials were erring on the side of strictness when in doubt.

On the other hand, the system of internal controls was open to criticism from the start and the manner in which those controls were put into effect was even more dubious. Army officials themselves found that the process of de-Nazification was not making much headway. The officers in direct charge of cities and towns were not carrying out the policy of their superiors in many instances, so far as that policy called for removal of all Third Reich advocates. Specific examples can be cited.

In Nuremberg, the top-ranking Allied officers in the economic field estimated that at least half of the principal officials of the local banks were active Nazis. Yet only 19 out of 318 of them were removed. The military had chosen as their liaison with German bankers the director of the Nuremberg Reichsbank, who had been active in various organizations affiliated with the Nazis.

Again, by order of the Allied command, the transport

system of western Germany was placed in the hands of former Reich Minister of Transport Dorpmuller, who had also been head of the German State Railways. He was empowered to nominate his subordinates. No doubt Dorpmuller and the Nuremberg bankers know their subjects well enough. They may even know them too well, and use their positions to sabotage the very aims that the occupation is designed to achieve.

It is bad enough to leave Nazis in posts of authority or responsibility, causing Germans as well as the rest of the world to wonder what we were fighting for. It is worse to help these men build up a new, strong Germany. Yet that is just what we are doing so far as we are assuming responsibility for the entire German economy.

We have all seen the tremendous machinery of government that is necessary to effect emergency economic controls—rationing, price ceilings and the rest. Even with the good will of most of the population, they have been difficult to operate in every warring nation. In Germany, the Allies began by taking too much responsibility for them, and their only hope of escaping a real, dangerous threat to their policy is by dropping that responsibility.

If it should suit the Germans to bring on an economic collapse which they could blame on their conquerors, it would be easy for them to destroy the whole structure of controls. Imagine trying to ration consumer goods against the active opposition of the whole population! Imagine price ceilings which every storekeeper and customer would consider it the height of patriotism to break! Imagine enforcing priority and wage regulations with all industry and labor conspiring to violate them! Imagine a fiscal system among a whole nation of tax evaders and inflation mongers! That is the situation the Germans could bring about any time they wanted to discredit detailed Allied control of their economy.

But failure would be a lesser evil than success. For success would mean a German recovery more rapid than anything that can be achieved by the nations attempting to prevent her from becoming a menace to peace again. This is no idle threat. On July 12, the Overseas News Agency carried a dispatch from Nuremberg, which said:

> With the approval of military government authorities and often backed by the influence of cash of American business, German heavy industry and electrical manufacturing plants are recovering at a dizzy pace. Germany is outstripping the United States in the reconversion race—reconversion solely for the benefit of Germany's reconstruction. . . . According to the local AMG, the general picture is this:
>
> Within three months, Nuremberg, one of the world's largest centers for the production of electrical appliances, railway cars and motor trucks, will be producing 80 per cent of its full capacity. Since no policy opposing this manufacture has been established, the industrial program for rebuilding Germany completely ignores the war-ravaged nations whose industries were looted and wrecked by the Nazis.

That sort of thing is inevitable as long as Allied military government is ordered or even allowed to consider itself responsible for Germany's industrial and commercial system. Once they have been given or have taken this responsibility, the Allied officers quite naturally want to do a good job. They will urge more help for the German civilian, and they will be listened to by their superiors with more sympathy and respect than German officials could command. The greater needs of liberated countries will not be so close to these Allied officers.

The bitterness and dissension which such tactics arouse among the despoiled nations to whom the United States promised its friendship and help must be one result of such a policy. An even more dangerous consequence will be the impetus given Germany to recapture her industrial hegemony of Europe.

The alternative is very clear. It is also comparatively simple. The five Allied controls which really can help achieve the over-all objective of peace—and are necessary to it—can be operated with a fraction of the staff that would be required to police the whole German economy.

The first one, control of political movements, can be met by the obvious requirement that all German governments must be acceptable to the occupying authorities. It would not be possible to prevent the existence of underground movements, but the open political life of the country can be observed and kept in line by a small staff.

The second, supervision of education, will require more personnel. It will be a long, arduous process to purge the schools, the press, the radio, the theater, the movies, the clubs and discussion groups of Nazi philosophies. But an international commission could make considerable strides in that direction.

Third is the machinery needed to prevent the production of the physical means of waging war. It would not take a large staff to make sure that Germany has no heavy industries. A steel mill, a synthetic rubber plant, a shipyard, an automobile assembly plant or a factory for making turbines cannot be hidden. The inspectors would not have to worry about what went on inside the walls. The mere existence of the building would be proof of violation. Reparations can be an excellent instrument of control. German machinery, for the basic materials of war can be an important addition—perhaps the most valuable feature of the reparations account.

The fourth job of keeping the German militarist from a conspiracy of war and revenge in other countries will present considerable difficulties. Every effort should be made to bar the emigration of key people in the Army, industry and research. Strict control over foreign trade, foreign exchange and foreign communications will be required. International business relations of Germans, the international German organizations of all kinds and German control over any foreign business have to be broken. All this will need a considerable amount of policing. But again, it is far less than that required for policing Germany's internal affairs.

Complete success in the fifth area of control, stamping out German scientific research for war, is not to be expected. But it can be hampered and its effectiveness greatly reduced by appropriate measures. Universities and industries should be forbidden to maintain research laboratories, and a relatively simple routine of inspection could insure general obedience. Hidden laboratories will still be possible, but not the more perilous and effective co-ordination of vast research projects.

In the beginning such a network of controls is likely to be quite efficient. The Allies approach the task with some enthusiasm. The Germans are relatively disorganized and helpless. But no control system is going to be either a cure-all or permanent. As the years go on, the commissions and the Allied peoples are bound to relax a little unless their zeal is maintained by something besides the routine of inspection in Germany.

We are neither much more intelligent nor much more moral than the generation that thought it had ended war forever in 1918. Our only advantage over them is that we have the benefit of their experience. That has taught us to distrust the efficacy of a piece of machinery which is not connected to any source of power. The apparatus for preventing German aggression can contain a set of economic and political and military controls. It will have to contain more—destruction of German heavy industry. But the whole thing will be inanimate, useless unless it is hooked up to the driving force of a strong and lasting United Nations will to peace.

Chapter XIV

GERMANY AND THE WORLD SECURITY ORGANIZATION

"WHEN YOU ASSEMBLE A NUMBER OF men to have the benefit of their joint wisdom, you inevitably assemble with those men all their prejudices, their passions, their errors of opinion, their local interests, and their selfish views."

So said Benjamin Franklin, perhaps the wisest man America ever produced. He was speaking to—and speaking of—the Constitutional Convention of 1787, that really wonderful group of creative thinkers who had just composed what Gladstone once called "the greatest work ever struck off at a given time by the brain and purpose of mankind." Franklin, eighty-one years old and very much the dean of that gathering, was not as greatly impressed as Gladstone was to be by the work he and his colleagues had done, but he pleaded for unanimous adoption of the Constitution on these grounds:

"From such an Assembly can a perfect production be expected? Thus I consent, Sir, to this Constitution because I expect no better, and because I am not sure it is not the best. The opinions I have had of its errors, I sacrifice to the public good."

The men who drew up the United Nations Charter were not more talented nor more farsighted nor more unselfish than the authors of the Constitution. They did not do a better job. But they knew that nothing less than international machinery to function as well in keeping world peace as our national government has done in insuring domestic tranquillity would satisfy war-weary peoples. In our time the biggest threat to peace has been Germany. Therefore the settlement of the German problem is the key to the success of United Nations plans for genuine security throughout the world.

There are several ways in which decisions taken about Germany will affect the world security organization. First of all, of course, is the simple fact that Germany, as one country in the world, must be the concern of any agency that proposes to deal with all the world. As the incorrigible disturbers of the peace in this century, Germany and Japan will be of especial importance to an organization dedicated to promoting peace. If Germany is again permitted to become one of the great industrial powers of the world, dominating all Europe or even any large part of it, she will be in a position to sabotage any attempt to continue international co-operation. She will be able to do it by playing off one member of the Security Council against another. If Germany is really disarmed, there will be a considerable body of opinion holding that the world agency should see to it that she stays that way.

However, the world agency was not formed to deal with Germany; rather Germany should be dealt with in a manner best calculated to serve the world agency. The distinction is an important one. It was not very clearly made at the Paris peace conference of 1919, and because it was not, Germany was able to add much to the difficulties and the frustrations of the League of Nations. If we are to consider the United Nations as now engaged in framing the equivalent of our Constitution, we can look back at the League Covenant as serving the purpose of our Articles of Confederation. Both were pretty dismal failures so far as accomplishing their main purposes were concerned. Both were carelessly dismissed as hopeless, the good features along with the bad. But the framers of the Constitution based a good deal of their work on the lessons they had learned under the Confederation. The men of San Francisco obviously learned a great deal from the League of Nations.

There was deliberate purpose at Paris in drafting the settlement in such a way that there were, as Wilson said, "so many threads of the Treaty tied to the Covenant that you cannot dissect the Covenant from the Treaty without destroying the whole vital structure." He was right, but the effect was not quite what he had anticipated. The whole vital structure was destroyed by desperate efforts to untangle the Covenant from the treaty and finally by the emergence of a newly armed and belligerent Germany. But the 1919 reasoning seemed very logical at the time. The League, Wilson argued, would be strengthened by the important tasks of enforcing details of the peace, by having the responsibility for the mandates over former German colonies and by practical jurisdiction over key points in Europe. These duties, he thought, would prevent the League from degenerating into a debating society.

It turned out in actual practice that the League was burdened with too much detail, was too intimately connected with treaty enforcement and finally was too weak to assert its authority in the field where it was most important for an international body to act. A study of the League's successes and failures gives a clear indication of the reasons for both.

Every session of the Assembly or the Council was bogged down in a mass of trifles which should never have been brought to Geneva at all. For instance, the Council hardly ever met without being confronted with some new question of administration in the so-called free city of Danzig. An organization whose duty was to maintain the peace of the world should have been above dealing with the petty governmental details of a Baltic port. Yet one meeting of the Council was treated to a lengthy, tedious debate over Poland's claim to have mailboxes in Danzig under her own control. It was difficult for the world to take too seriously the deliberations of statesmen who concerned themselves with such minutiae while the real problems of disarmament and economic aggression went unsolved.

The League's prestige suffered, too, from being considered as an instrument for enforcing the Versailles Treaty. Wilson's own highest hopes for it were that it would become an agency through which the 1919 settlement, whose imperfections he recognized as clearly as anyone else of his day, could be amended, changed and improved. Actually, many of the League's friends as well as its enemies thought that its principal duty was to see that the Versailles terms were carried out in every detail. They looked upon the League as a combination traffic policeman and booking clerk when it could only succeed by being a combination Supreme Court justice and prime minister.

In the broad fields where it was successful, in the formation of the International Labor Organization and the war on the drug traffic, for example, the League was operating in areas where the treaty did not get in its way. It was blazing new trails in international procedure, and virtually all nations, including our own, co-operated with it to achieve success.

Translating this experience into the current problem of what to do with Germany, it becomes plain that an augury of hope for the world security organization is that it need not be saddled with enforcement of details or be subjected to German intrigues for more lenient treatment. It would be concerned only with a German question if the Reich threatens the peace. And the world agency will have a much better chance to get itself firmly established if this question is not allowed to arise.

Therefore, the real disarmament of Germany through prohibition of the means for rearmament will remove one hurdle from the path of true international co-operation. Germany's smaller neighbors will be reassured. Her larger neighbors will not find themselves in conflict with more remote Allies because of differences of opinion as to whether the Reich has again become a menace to them. Russia will not have to fear that the western powers are building up Germany as a bulwark against her. England and France will not be tortured with nightmares (such as that which plagued Lloyd George) of German technical skill marshaling Russian resources against them.

"The sovereign equality of all its members" was written

into the charter very carefully. It is the basis for the co-operation of small countries as well as large. But full sovereignty is impossible under the shadow of a powerful and aggressive neighbor. Until the power of the world agency is as well established as that of individual great nations, the countries of Central Europe and the Balkans particularly will be tempted to weigh a powerful Germany against the untried might of the world agency. The result of such an appraisal may well be their reluctant return to the German orbit, for the world agency will have failed to inspire a feeling of security. Such a feeling would be the beginning of the old disastrous cycle of economic concessions, military concessions, secret treaties of "mutual assistance" and war.

These smaller nations could co-operate much more wholeheartedly for peace if their fear of Germany were removed. Some of their spokesmen have already plainly indicated that for the present they would prefer security to prosperity because the prosperity cannot last without the security. But the larger nations would be equally apprehensive.

Whether a powerful Germany be excluded from the world organization or admitted to it, the danger to peace would be equally great, until that remote day comes when the rest of the world can be sure that Germany's fervor for war has been eliminated. Outside the organization, Germany would work alternately on the fears of East and West, promising her support to each in turn against the other. Inside the organization, she would be a disruptive force confusing the public mind and stirring honest differences of opinion into grounds for suspicion and hate.

On the other hand, a Germany deprived of her heavy industry as a means of rearming would be not only less inclined to create international disturbances but would have little ability to do so. In all probability any war thus aroused would be fought over her territory, so she would have a real incentive to avert it. Her smaller neighbors could act as their true interests, and not their fears, dictate. Russia, England and France would find that their interests are complementary, not antagonistic, in the absence of any threat from rearmed Germany. All of them, great and small alike, would be more confident of the protection to be gained by co-operation for peace.

All this points to certain specific conclusions in the relation of the world security agency to Germany. The measures for genuine disarmament of the Reich must be taken by the United Nations as allies in war, not as partners in peace. The elimination of heavy industry, the controls over German foreign trade and foreign communications, the transfer of populations, the international administration of the Ruhr, the partition of the rest of Germany, the punishment of war criminals, the elimination of Nazi and Pan-German influences from politics, education and communications, reparations—all these and other details of the settlement with Germany should be the responsibility of the Allies. They should not burden a new organization, which will have plenty of other work of its own, with these essentially war measures. The new organization is to be concerned with preparing the new paths to peace, not with resurfacing the bomb-pitted road to war.

The world security organization can then proceed with

its real work without being torn by dissension over the details of this or that section of the treatment of Germany. It will not have to debate who controls the letter boxes in the Ruhr. It will not have to consider whether the boundary between Germany and Poland runs along the right bank or the left bank of a stream. It will not have to decide whether some family in East Prussia has been properly compensated for the goods it left behind when it moved back to Germany. It will not have to pass upon the fate of some obscure German criminal claimed by both Czechoslovakia and Belgium. Such problems could only divert it from the main business of establishing the working machinery for peace.

At present, furthermore, the sole power for enforcing decisions on Germany is in the hands of the Allied armies. It is always a mistake to divorce responsibility from power. If the world security organization is given the duty of carrying out the terms of the settlement with Germany, both the success of the organization and the fulfillment of the terms will be jeopardized. Germans will soon learn that the world agency has no force of its own to back up its decisions. Evasion will then become much easier and more attractive to them. Any protests by the world agency will have to be referred to the Allies for transmittal to their commanders of the armies of occupation. That immediately places the agency in a position subservient to individual nations.

On the other hand, if the responsibility is lodged where the power lies, action can be taken more promptly and more efficiently. Therefore, there is less likelihood that it will have to be taken at all. German failure to destroy a synthetic gasoline plant will not have to be referred to an advisory body outside Germany. The United Nations commissions and commanders on the spot will have the authority and duty to blow it up themselves. The world agency's work in organizing a system of peace will not have to be interrupted by the referral of some complaint that a German firm has been violating exchange regulations or is building up a research laboratory abroad. The allied control commission will deal with the German violator on its own.

Under these conditions, the world agency can deal with Germany in the same way as it deals with any other country. Only the German share in the over-all peace picture will be of interest or concern to the Security Council or the International Court. The Germans and we ourselves will come to look upon it as a higher and more important entity in the establishment of universal security, for it will be able to maintain a perspective as wide as all the earth, not narrowed to the particular problems of a defeated Germany.

Chapter XV

BRING THE MEN HOME

"THESE KRAUTS AIN'T SO BAD!"

The words, uttered by an American soldier who had just been presented with a glass of beer, a smile from a pretty girl and a flower from a small child, sum up the reason why United States troops should not be a part of the long-term army of occupation in Germany. The unidentified private who expressed this opinion in tones indicating a pleasant surprise was one of the first to enter Cologne. He shared the views of many thousands.

A day or two later, one of his comrades, Sergeant Francis Mitchell, explained to newspapermen why Americans could not hold much of a grudge against their civilian enemies. The sergeant had been fighting hard for weeks, but without a great deal of hate in his heart. He was doing a hard job efficiently. He knew from reading and from talking that the Nazis were guilty of horrible brutalities. But he could not connect these bloody excesses with the smiling, apparently friendly people in Cologne. He said he and his fellows just hadn't been trained to resist kindness from a good-looking fräulein or a motherly woman or a gentle old man or a wistful child. He thought it was very pleasant that young women offered him beer, that housewives gave him food, that all the people cheered and waved as if they were being liberated.

Americans are pretty proud of fellows like Sergeant Francis Mitchell. It is good to know that they can fight so well and not lose the sympathy for others, the response to kindness and the consideration that makes them good citizens. Bitter and brutal experiences have neither embittered nor brutalized them. But by the same token it has not equipped them to appraise the significance of the German reaction to their presence. It is quite natural for the average Germans to become meek and inoffensive characters to all appearances whenever they are confronted with soldiers or the obvious label of arbitrary authority. It is not conscious hypocrisy that makes them anxious to please a conqueror, fawning and a little subservient, for they have been trained in obedience to force rather than in obedience to justice.

No men in the armies of the United Nations are likely to be so susceptible as Americans to the danger of this people's bid for compassion. The misery of hunger and cold is bound to be extreme in Germany this winter. Until the workers in her heavy industry and her demobilized soldiers have begun to raise food crops and rebuild houses, there will be malnutrition and exposure for their people. The only possible way to avoid it would be to divert food and materials and labor from other European nations even more in need of them.

But the American soldier in the army of occupation has not seen the devastation of Poland and Russia, Yugoslavia and Greece, Norway and Czechoslovakia. He has seen little of the suffering of France, Belgium and Holland, and may well look upon that little as the inevitable destruction of the battlefield. In his heart he compares the lot of Germans with the lot of the city or town or countryside from which he came in the States. The tendency is for him to believe the Germans are more destitute and miserable than any other people. They are sure to tell him so. Soon he will become, if he is not now, a ready victim to a campaign for more lenient treatment of Germany.

On the other hand, the argument that it is more important to feed Greeks than Germans seems extremely logical to a Greek soldier. It is not difficult to persuade a French poilu that it is better to keep French homes warm this winter than provide fuel for German homes. It seems only just to a Russian infantryman that Russian cities get material for reconstruction rather than that German factories be rebuilt. Stories of continued shortages in their own home communities harden British, Belgian, Dutch and other troops against the demands of Germans to have their own shortages relieved.

Therefore, it is not merely a sentimental desire to get our own men back that prompts the proposal that they should leave Germany soon. The tasks in which they should participate need not take long. They should help supervise the complete disarmament of the Reich. They might be on hand to hasten the dismantling of German heavy industry. Then they should give way to the troops of our European Allies.

The only Americans remaining in Germany should be our members of those boards and commissions which will deal with the various aspects of control, and our share of the technicians needed to carry out the work. There should be no line officers, combat troops or administrative officers of the AMG; the routine of this sort of occupation can be done by the troops of Germany's European neighbors.

The same argument applies to all other non-European troops. Besides the Americans, the United Nations should withdraw the soldiers of Canada, Australia and South Africa, and the Dutch, Belgian and French colonials. No occupying army should be left in Germany without arranging for frequent leaves to keep the troops in touch with their own country and people. This can be managed for the French, Russians and British; it will not be possible for men from other parts of the world.

The history of the American occupation of the Rhineland after World War I illustrates the dangers that would be confronted if a new, long-term American army of occupation is formed now. Twenty-five years ago, the Americans, homesick and bored and without very much to do, were subjected to a barrage of German propaganda. German sufferings were intruded upon their notice and greatly exaggerated.

"Germany is on the verge of starvation," cried the German Armistice Commission. "The harsh armistice terms of the Allies merely precipitated this tragedy. Famine leads to anarchy and Bolshevism, which now menace Germany."

"The German food supply is on the brink of a catastrophe," mourned the *Vossische Zeitung* on December 15, 1918. "The decision remains with our enemies whether they will pay the price to save Germany from hunger and anarchy."

"If," warned the *Vorwaerts*, "we do not succeed in giving food, light, heat, shelter and clothing to the people, despite the frightful difficulty in maintaining communications, then we are lost, because first comes hunger, then anarchy, civil warfare, the fall of the state, and on the heels of this, the intervention of a merciless enemy."

Actually the Germans were a great deal better off than a great many other peoples of Europe. Colonel I. L. Hunt, officer in charge of civil affairs in the Rhineland during the occupation, considered the German estimates of the food situation grossly exaggerated. He said:

> That there was a considerable shortage of foods, particularly those to which the German was accustomed, and of food luxuries, cannot be denied, but that seventy million people were on the verge of starvation is untrue. It is perfectly true that the comparative scarcity of accustomed articles of food, and the probability of the condition becoming more pronounced, was producing an ever-increasing social unrest. This is particularly so, as the condition was depicted in more or less exaggerated form and constantly held before the people in public print.

Nevertheless, the German propaganda was effective among our own troops of occupation. In April, 1919, the United States Army began the sale of flour from army stocks at cost prices to the civilian population. Later bacon, sugar, rice, lard, canned beef, salmon and milk were similarly furnished. At the time, the hunger Germany complained about, but was not actually experiencing, was a horrible reality in Central Europe. Even neutral Scandinavians were undernourished because they could not yet get supplies from abroad. The Army explained that its distribution in Germany was made "in order to allay the social unrest due to scarcity or impending scarcity of food, and to the nondistribution of allotted supplies." The "impending scarcity" was German propaganda; the failure to distribute allotted supplies was the fault of the Germans, if it existed.

Another feature of the American occupation was the inability of the Army to prevent fraternization between its soldiers and the German civilians. Whenever one loophole was closed, another was discovered. A month after the Armistice, the first of a long series of anti-fraternization orders was issued. The difficulties of enforcement were illustrated by a civil affairs officer's report on the reasons for suspending the first order.

> When the Army of Occupation had been dissolved, the combat troops returned to the States, and only the permanent garrison remained, [he explained]. The troops were no longer billeted on inhabitants where they could enjoy the feminine society of the household, but were lodged in barracks. They could meet no women legally, and the only ones who would risk meeting them in violation of orders were the lowest type of prostitutes. The result was that the venereal rate, which had been surprisingly small during the time of the Army of Occupation, now grew amazingly large. In the hope of correcting this, the Commanding General determined to revoke the anti-fraternization order, in order that soldiers might again associate with decent women. Accordingly, on September 27, 1919, an Administrative Bulletin No. 52 revoked the anti-fraternization order.

Evidently the new policy reduced the venereal disease rate, but it was followed by an epidemic of requests for permission to marry German women. A new set of restrictions was imposed, the Commanding General explaining:

"The numerous excess of good-looking marriageable girls in this zone over corresponding German males accentuated the necessity of adopting the policy cited to avoid having a partially Germanized command."

There are better ways of checking venereal disease among our troops than marrying them off to German girls or even permitting them to "associate with decent women." One way is to bring them home, and leave the police work to troops who can be given furloughs to go back to their own countries and meet their own women.

Nobody wants Americans to behave so that they will be cordially hated in the lands through which they pass. But the whole purpose of an army of occupation is to enforce unpalatable terms. That the American troops were not very good at this is evidenced by the appeal of the German Foreign Minister against withdrawal of the Americans from the Rhineland in 1922. They were to be replaced by other Allied forces. Secretary of State Hughes received from the German Foreign Minister a note protesting the change because it would remove the "impartial and moderating influence of the American power of occupation." A report of the Assistant Chief of Staff, G-2, summed up the popular German reaction:

> The departure of a train filled with soldiers bound for the United States furnished evidence of the friendly relations. . . . The sight of the throngs of Germans gathered about the train, of the sorrowful and in some cases tear-stained countenances, and the shouted farewells made it difficult to realize that those leaving were soldiers of an army of occupation or that the crowds were composed of inhabitants of an occupied area.

A dozen years later those same sorrowing, tearful Germans were busily and openly preparing for another war, convinced that the Americans were a foolish degenerate lot who could never rouse themselves in time to meet a real danger.

This time the occupation is at once harder and more heart-rending. Allied troops are not confined to the Rhineland. They are not, as in 1918, stationed in cities virtually untouched by war. This time, there may well be real hunger, not just "impending scarcity of food." Millions of demobilized Germans have been returning to bombed-out homes and wrecked places of business. The sanitation and health conditions seem intolerable to an American.

Besides the pressure which our men's sympathy might create to divert supplies from countries even more devastated than Germany, there is a danger of weakening necessary controls for which the armies of occupation are a guarantee. To an American soldier it may well seem unfair that an apparently goodhearted German who has fed him beer and a hard luck story should not get a little piece of machinery from abroad. It may well seem harsh that an unhappy businessman should not smuggle out a few concealed assets to a brother in Argentina or Switzerland. The American may be persuaded much more easily than a Frenchman or an Englishman or a Russian to turn the other way from sheer goodness of heart while the transaction is completed. That very transaction may be a strong link in the chain leading to the rebuilding of Germany for another war.

The European's memory of five years of starvation is not so short nor so easily discarded as the American's recollection of his war training and combat. It is quite natural that the European has the more fixed determination to carry through a realistic program to prevent future German aggression. It is not an unusual citizen whose father was killed at the front between 1914 and 1918. If during this war his mother was bombed out of her home only once by the Luftwaffe, she would be considered lucky. His wife and children have been deprived of everything they owned, driven from one place to another like cattle, suffered years of malnutrition. They are accounted the fortunate ones among their acquaintances, for many families have been tortured and murdered by the Germans or perhaps taken off to Germany to serve in virtual slavery.

These men are not likely to be very susceptible to German pleadings of the 1920 model, nor even similar assaults upon their sympathy in the streamlined manner of more modern propaganda. It is no reflection upon the good sense of the American that he might be inclined to fall for it. His experience has not fitted him, any more than it has fitted his relatives at home, to carry out a cold, unfriendly but entirely necessary program. For most Americans, the realities of German aggression have been kept pretty far off. We have read about them, we have seen some of the victims, we have given up pleasure driving and better cuts of meat. We have worked as we never worked before, but on the whole the hardships of war for us have been transmuted largely into inconveniences.

Any permanent army of occupation we provide would share the same sentiments and the same experiences. For it would come fresh from those experiences. It would be too cruel to staff that army with the troops who have borne the brunt of the fighting. The whole country will agree that men who struggled ashore at Algiers and Anzio and Normandy, who chased Rommel through North Africa and Italy and pursued von Rundstedt across France, Belgium and Germany should not go back a year or so later for garrison duty in the Reich. So our army of occupation would have to be composed of new recruits from home. Yet even the most hardened of our warriors, who can be very grim in combat, have already proved that they do not make very enduring enemies. The stories of fraternization that came promptly from the American zone in Germany were inevitable. The same spirit in higher ranks prompted a recommendation that German coal miners be allowed a larger food ration (which would have to be filled from army stocks). The ration proposed by these officials figured out at a little higher than the ration allowed a French miner at the same time. And already we have heard quite a good deal about the food shortages in Germany, although virtually all observers comment on how much better fed the Germans look than do the people they oppressed for five years of Nazi occupation. American soldiers have been, perhaps, the most affected by the tales of the people among whom they are quartered.

The whole difference in the psychology of our people and those of the Continent in these matters was summed up very concisely by a European exile, who reported perhaps a little enviously:

> The most outstanding fact of American life is that an American couple may proceed with the business of raising a family with some confidence that their home will not become a battleground and that their life endeavors

will not be swept away by war. No European can ever have such confidence.

The disinclination to have American troops share in the routine of policing occupied Germany is no reflection of a desire to withdraw from American responsibilities and privileges in helping to maintain the peace of the world. The great majority of the American people are eager to have their country play its full part on the international stage. But the development of a peaceful world calls for each nation to contribute what it can best perform. The duties of an army of occupation in Germany are not the role Americans are best suited to act. Europeans readily understand that, and will be quite satisfied to provide the men, if our co-operation is indicated by membership on the commissions which set policy, on the technical staffs which try to carry it out and on the high military command.

It is no aspersion on the American soldier to adjudge him too inexperienced in the ways of international banditry to serve as a guard in the German reformatory. The misfortunes of Europe have put its soldiers through the cruel and bitter course of training which fits them to serve most efficiently in the surveillance of Germany. They are willing and able to do the job. Americans can be content with the honor their men have won in the incomparable fight they have fought—and bring them home.

Chapter XVI

PARTNERS IN PEACE

PEACE IS INDIVISIBLE. THE GERMAN solution is only one of the factors that cannot be separated from the others. None of them will be achieved without the lasting determination of the people of the United Nations to have peace nor without their continuing interest in the measures that strengthen it and the measures that threaten it. For peace is won or lost in the last analysis by the people themselves. There is no other kind of peace except a people's peace.

This is no new discovery in the world. It has been recognized by the most widely varying schools of unfettered political philosophy. Here are two carefully thought out expressions of opinion on the subject:

> In differences between nations which go beyond the limited range of arbitrable questions, peace can only be maintained by putting behind it the force of united nations determined to uphold it and prevent war.... It might easily be said that this idea, which is not a new one, is impracticable; but it is better than the idea that war can be stopped by language, by speechmaking, by vain agreements, which no one would carry out when the stress came, by denunciations of war and laudations of peace, in which all men agree.... It may seem Utopian at this moment to suggest a union of civilized nations in order to put a controlling force behind the maintenance of peace and international order.... At all events, it is along this path that we must travel if we

> are to attain in any measure to the end we all desire of peace upon earth.

And:

> If the peace presently made is to endure, it must be a peace made secure by the organized major force of mankind. . . . I can predict with absolute certainty that within another generation there will be another world war if the nations of the world do not concert the method by which to prevent it. . . . I do not hesitate to say that the war we have just been through, though it was shot through with terror of every kind, is not to be compared with the war we would have to face next time. . . . What the Germans used were toys as compared with what would be used in the next war. . . . Settlements may be temporary, but the action of the nations in the interest of peace and justice must be permanent. We can set up permanent processes. We may not be able to set up permanent decisions. . . . A steadfast concert for peace can never be maintained except by a partnership of democratic nations. No autocratic government could be trusted to keep faith within it or observe its covenants.

These things sound like speeches made at the San Francisco conference of the United Nations. But they are a bit older than that. The first are the words of Henry Cabot Lodge! Woodrow Wilson spoke the second set.

The world may well wonder how two men of such similar ideals for peace came to disagree so profoundly over the actual machinery that was set up in 1919 to achieve it. Such speculation is a pleasant historical exercise, and has been indulged in a good deal during the last few years. It also has some practical value for the men who are making the peace now. The things on which Wilson and

Lodge agreed seem and are of overwhelming importance to us today, so much so that the words they used sound as contemporary as last night's radio commentators. But their differences are as remote as Cicero's orations to the Roman Senate. For the forms and phrases are simply the layers of cotton wool in which the jeweler swaths a precious gem. They are thrown away and forgotten, but underneath them is the diamond, flashing and brilliant and lasting.

The postwar world is not going to be an easy one. The years of struggle and selfishness into which all the nations sank after 1918, the bitter intolerance and hatreds which were bequeathed by depression and aggression, the final years of terrible destruction in war have left a heritage of ruins. The tangle of international relations has been doubly confounded by the shattering impact of total war on one country after another throughout the world. Men of orderly minds may well feel themselves lost in the maze and wonder despairingly where there is any guide out of the labyrinth. But there are guides. Several threads, if only they are kept in the hands of peoples stumbling toward the light, can lead us out of darkness. They consist of a few relatively simple principles.

One of them, a hard one to keep a grip upon when powerful advocates are contending against each other, is that the forms by which we achieve peace are not very important when stacked up against the goal we want to achieve. For instance, the United States and the British Commonwealth have worked out democratic systems that are in form altogether different. We base ours upon a written Constitution and the equality of all men. The

British, with an hereditary monarchy and aristocracy, have no written constitution at all. They get along in a democratic way about as well as we do—almost any Englishman will say better. The feature that makes both of these governments function effectively is not a matter of form at all but the fundamental fact that they are responsible to the people. On the other hand, beautiful models of democracy, like the Weimar constitution, have proved a farce. This truth is not confined to national affairs. It will be as valid in the development of the world security organization, and quibbles over form can have no effect save to postpone the day when war will be preventable.

Second on the list of principles is the will to peace. A small fraction of the patient, determined preparation which went into the war would be enough to establish security from war. The governments of the world will remain alert and active in the pursuit of peace only so long as their peoples have an equal interest. It is a good working hypothesis that no government can long survive the opposition of an overwhelming majority of its constituents. A strong, vital popular demand for peace will keep it every time. It sounds easy. But it has proved beyond the power of mankind up to now. Domestic problems loom so large and so close! In 1931, when jobs were vanishing along with bank accounts and homes and enough clothes to keep the children decent at school, it would have required an enormous effort of will to get people to devote as much attention to Japan's occupation of Manchuria as to stock market quotations in New York. What they actually did was to accuse Secretary of State Henry L. Stimson of "warmongering" when he proposed to Britain that we do something about it. Yet that faraway incident touched off the whole series of events that led straight to world war. The will was lacking, and the Axis tide of conquest was the result. Determination could have stopped it in 1931. The lives of millions of the world's finest men have been barely enough to stop it now.

Third on our list is tolerance. A cardinal point of virtually every religion, it has been most honored in the breach for two thousand years. Of course, tolerance does not mean winking at evil. But it does mean respect for the rights of others, and more than that, a willingness to enforce respect for those rights. It is no trouble at all to get up a pretty big indignation meeting to protest against the denial of free speech to an orator who was going to expound a doctrine in which the indignant ones believe. It is a bit more unusual to find any large number of Democrats roused to a pitch of fighting fury by the refusal of a Mississippi audience to hear a Republican explain the virtues of his party. The National Association of Manufacturers can work up a dignified sweat over a brush-off for their spokesman by a Congressional committee. It views with Olympian calm the expulsion of a labor organizer from a factory town. Similarly any labor union can easily call together a well-attended meeting for a rousing protest against that expulsion. But its members would be inclined to smile over the fate of the NAM spokesman. Now that sort of tolerance is dangerous enough in domestic affairs. But we have the traditions and the enforceable laws to keep it from getting too far out of hand. It is fatal in international dealings. The nations of the world must be prepared to enforce respect for the rights, the real rights of countries they compete with or whose forms of government they do not especially admire.

Mankind has been very ingenious in devising complexities to endanger its collective existence. It has thought up whole libraries of different languages, philosophies and religions, and has gone to war about them. It has thought up spheres of influence, imperialistic "manifest destinies" and baffling claims to other people's property, and has gone to war about them. It has thought up economic discriminations, trade rivalries and monopolistic empires, and has gone to war about them, too.

But not one of the so-called causes of war could fail to yield to a combination of tolerance for the rights of others, determination to see that peace is maintained and almost any fairly easily understood machinery for enforcing the peace. In fact, the union of those three principles is an unbeatable hand. It would make the peoples of the world, not just their governments, what they most aspire to be in their hearts—genuine partners in peace.

Appendix A

STATISTICS ON GERMAN FOOD PRODUCTION, CONSUMPTION AND IMPORTS

TABLE I

SUPPLIES FROM LOCAL RESOURCES AVAILABLE FOR HUMAN CONSUMPTION IN OLD AND NEW GERMANY*

(1,000 METRIC TONS)

	Supplies from local resources available for human consumption for all Germany 1943-1944	Amount produced in areas to be ceded 1943-1944	Per cent produced in areas to be ceded
Bread grain	9,644	1,431	14.8
Sugar	1,596	239	14.9
Beef and veal	1,007	137	13.6
Pork	832	118	14.1
Pig fat	208	30	14.4
Fresh milk	4,200	526	12.5
Butter	630	92	14.6
Cheese	240	35	14.5

* "New Germany" is used here to describe that territory which will remain in the German states after such a partition as is described in Chapter XII, not that outlined in the Berlin Declaration.

TABLE II

The German Diet
1933-1937
(Consumption per capita per day)

	Protein (grams)	Fat (grams)	Carbohydrate (grams)	Calories
Breadstuffs and cereals, including rice, in terms of flour	23.9	2.3	215.0	1,004
Potatoes	6.3	0.5	84.9	378
Sugar	...	...	58.6	240
Dry legumes	1.0	...	2.9	16
Fresh vegetables	2.0	0.3	7.3	40
Fruits	0.7	0.3	15.0	66
Nuts	0.3	1.2	0.2	13
Fats and oils	0.1	64.9	0.1	604
Meat and poultry	24.3	19.8	...	256
Fish	3.2	2.0	...	32
Eggs	2.0	1.9	0.1	27
Milk	10.8	12.5	16.2	226
Cheese	2.8	2.8	0.4	39
Alcohol	0.9	...	4.8	75
Cocoa	0.2	0.7	0.9	11
Honey	...	...	0.8	3
Totals	78.5	109.2	407.2	3,030

TABLE III

German Consumption of Foodstuffs in Calories 1933-1937

	Average daily total per capita caloric intake	Per cent of total per capita caloric intake	Average daily per capita caloric intake derived from domestic production
Breadstuffs	1,004	33.1	984.9
Potatoes	378	12.5	378.0
Sugar	240	7.9	240.0
Dry legumes	16	0.5	9.8
Fresh vegetables	40	1.3	36.9
Fruits	66	2.2	48.2
Nuts	13	0.4	4.1
Fats and oils	604	19.9	352.1
Meat and poultry	256	8.4	247.6
Fish	32	1.2	23.1
Eggs	27	0.9	21.3
Milk	226	7.5	226.0
Cheese	39	1.2	34.2
Raw cocoa	11	0.4	78.0 (Raw cocoa, Honey, Alcohol combined)
Honey	3	0.1	
Alcohol	75	2.5	
Totals	3,030	100.0	2,684.2

TABLE IV

ESTIMATED DOMESTIC PRODUCTION, NET IMPORTS, AND CONSUMPTION OF FOODSTUFFS. AVERAGE 1938-1937

(in thousands metric tons)

	Domestic production for food Average 1933-1937	Net imports for consumption Average 1933-1937	Total domestic consumption	Per cent imported 1933-1937
Breadstuff and cereals, including rice, in terms of flour	7,100	135	7,235	1.9
Potatoes	12,700	...	12,700	...
Sugar	1,450	...	1,450	...
Dry legumes	156	100	256	39.0
Fresh vegetables	3,000	250	3,250	7.7
Fruits	2,300	850	3,150	27.0
Nuts	18	39	57	68.4
Fats and oils (edible only)	1,000	714	1,714	41.7
Meats and poultry	3,081	106	3,187	3.3
Fish	557	214	771	27.8
Eggs	357	95	452	21.0
Whole milk, fresh	8,260	...	8,260	...
Cheese	300	42	342	12.3

Appendix B

STATISTICS ON GERMAN EMPLOYMENT

TABLE 1

INDUSTRIAL EMPLOYMENT IN GERMANY, 1933-1939

Industry Group	June, 1933	June, 1939	Rate of Increase 1933-1939 Per cent
	Number of Persons Employed		
Mining	500,000	690,000	38
Quarries	400,000	750,000	87
Iron and steel	275,000	640,000	133
Metal foundries and semi-finished metal products	50,000	120,000	133*
Iron, steel and metal products	600,000	1,050,000	76
Machinery (except electrical) and transportation equipment	620,000	1,850,000	196
Electrical machinery	250,000	600,000	140
Optical products	100,000	230,000	130
Chemicals and allied products	250,000	400,000	59
Textile-mill products	850,000	1,000,000	20
Paper and allied products	190,000	200,000*	
Printing and allied industries	275,000	300,000*	
Leather and leather products	120,000	200,000*	
Rubber and rubber products	50,000	150,000*	
Sawmills, furniture and miscellaneous wooden goods	610,000	1,050,000	70
Musical instruments	40,000	50,000*	
Food and kindred products	1,450,000	1,600,000*	
Apparel and other fabricated textile products	1,050,000	1,550,000	46
Construction	1,025,000	4,000,000	290
Public utilities	150,000	200,000	
Laundering, cleaning and dyeing services	320,000	350,000	
Total	9,155,000	16,980,000	

* Estimated.

TABLE 2

EMPLOYMENT IN VARIOUS MANUFACTURING INDUSTRIES, GERMANY
June, 1933 and June, 1939
(Number of Employed Persons)

Industry Group	North German State		South German State		International Zone		Total	
	1933	1939	1933	1939	1933	1939	1933	1939
Iron and steel	35,720	85,000	11,956	27,600	175,022	410,000	522,500	967,896
Metal foundries and semifinished metal products	21,242	50,000	7,139	17,000	19,303	45,000	47,684	112,000
Iron, steel and metal products	197,399	350,000	135,504	240,000	189,698	335,000	522,601	925,000
Machinery (except electrical) and transportation equipment	261,706	775,000	137,249	410,000	158,376	470,000	557,331	1,655,000
Electrical machinery	133,372	320,000	49,336	120,000	51,543	125,000	234,251	565,000
Chemicals and allied products	104,687	165,000	39,367	65,000	68,981	110,000	213,035	340,000
Total	754,116	1,745,000	370,551	879,500	662,923	1,495,000	2,542,798	4,119,500

Appendix C

THE POTSDAM DECLARATION

For purposes of comparison with the program outlined in this book, the text of the Potsdam Declaration is presented herewith, as it appeared in the New York *Times*, August 3, 1945.

I. Report on the Tripartite Conference of Berlin

On July 17, 1945, the President of the United States of America, Harry S. Truman; the Chairman of the Council of People's Commissars of the Union of Soviet Socialist Republics, Generalissimo J. V. Stalin, and the Prime Minister of Great Britain, Winston S. Churchill, together with Mr. Clement R. Attlee, met in the Tripartite Conference of Berlin. They were accompanied by the Foreign Secretaries of the three Governments, Mr. Jamest F. Byrnes, Mr. V. M. Molotoff, and Mr. Anthony Eden, the Chief of Staff, and other advisers.

There were nine meetings between July 17 and July 25. The Conference was then interrupted for two days while the results of the British general election were being declared.

On July 28 Mr. Attlee returned to the Conference as Prime Minister, accompanied by the new Secretary of State for Foreign Affairs, Mr. Ernest Bevin. Four days of further discussion then took place. During the course of the Conference there were regular meetings of the heads of the three Governments accompanied by the Foreign Secretaries, and also of the Foreign Secretaries alone. Committees appointed by the Foreign Secretaries for preliminary consideration of questions before the Conference also met daily.

The meetings of the Conference were held at the Cecilienhof, near Potsdam. The Conference ended on Aug. 2, 1945.

Important decisions and agreements were reached. Views were exchanged on a number of other questions and consideration of these matters will be continued by the Council of Foreign Ministers, established by the Conference.

President Truman, Generalissimo Stalin and Prime Minister Attlee leave this Conference, which has strengthened the ties between the three Governments and extended the scope of their collaboration and understanding, with renewed confidence that their Governments and peoples, together with the other United Nations, will insure the creation of a just and enduring peace.

II. Establishment of a Council of Foreign Ministers

The Conference reached an agreement for the establishment of a Council of Foreign Ministers representing the five principal powers to continue the necessary preparatory work for the peace settlements and to take up other matters which from time to time may be referred to the Council by agreement of the Governments participating in the Council.

The text of the agreement for the establishment of the Council of Foreign Ministers is as follows:

1. There shall be established a Council composed of the Foreign Ministers of the United Kingdom, the Union of the Soviet Socialist Republics, China, France and the United States.

2. (I) The Council shall normally meet in London, which shall be the permanent seat of the Joint Secretariat which the Council will form. Each of the Foreign Ministers will be accompanied by a high-ranking deputy, duly authorized to carry on the work of the Council in the absence of his Foreign Minister, and by a small staff of technical advisers.

(II) The first meeting of the Council shall be held in London not later than Sept. 1, 1945. Meetings may be held by common agreement in other capitals as may be agreed from time to time.

3. (I) As its immediate important task the Council shall be authorized to draw up, with a view to their submission

to the United Nations, treaties of peace with Italy, Rumania, Bulgaria, Hungary and Finland, and to propose settlements of territorial questions outstanding on the termination of the war in Europe. The Council shall be utilized for the preparation of a peace settlement for Germany to be accepted by the government of Germany when a government adequate for the purpose is established.

(II) For the discharge of each of these tasks the Council will be composed of the members representing those states which were signatory to the terms of surrender imposed upon the enemy state concerned. For the purpose of the peace settlement for Italy, France shall be regarded as a signatory to the terms of surrender for Italy. Other members will be invited to participate when matters directly concerning them are under discussion.

(III) Other matters may from time to time be referred to the Council by agreement between the member Governments.

4. (I) Whenever the Council is considering a question of direct interest to a State not represented thereon, such State should be invited to send representatives to participate in the discussion and study of that question.

(II) The Council may adapt its procedure to the particular problem under consideration. In some cases it may hold its own preliminary discussions prior to the participation of other interested states. In other cases, the Council may convoke a formal conference of the state chiefly interested in seeking a solution of the particular problem.

In accordance with the decision of the Conference the three Governments have each addressed an identical invitation to the Governments of China and France to adopt this text and to join in establishing the Council.

The establishment of the Council of Foreign Ministers for the specific purposes named in the text will be without prejudice to the agreement of the Crimea conference that there should be periodic consultation among the foreign secretaries of the United States, the Union of Soviet Socialist Republics and the United Kingdom.

The conference also considered the position of the European Advisory Commission in the light of the agreement to establish the Council of Foreign Ministers. It was noted with satisfaction that the commission had ably discharged its principal task by the recommendations that it had furnished for the terms of Germany's unconditional surrender, for the zones of occupation in Germany and Austria, and for the inter-Allied control machinery in those countries. It was felt that further work of a detailed character for the coordination of Allied policy for the control of Germany and Austria would in future fall within the competence of the Allied control council at Berlin and the Allied commission at Vienna. Accordingly, it was agreed to recommend that the European Advisory Commission be dissolved.

III. Germany

The Allied armies are in occupation of the whole of Germany and the German people have begun to atone for the terrible crimes committed under the leadership of those whom in the hour of their success, they openly approved and blindly obeyed.

Agreement has been reached at this conference on the political and economic principles of a coordinated Allied policy toward defeated Germany during the period of Allied control.

The purpose of this agreement is to carry out the Crimea Declaration on Germany. German militarism and nazism will be extirpated and the Allies will take in agreement together, now and in the future, the other measures necessary to assure that Germany never again will threaten her neighbors or the peace of the world.

It is not the intention of the Allies to destroy or enslave the German people. It is the intention of the Allies that the German people be given the opportunity to prepare for the eventual reconstruction of their life on a democratic and peaceful basis. If their own efforts are steadily directed to this end, it will be possible for them in due course to take their place among the free and peaceful peoples of the world.

The text of the agreement is as follows:

The political and economic principles to govern the treatment of Germany in the initial control period.

A. POLITICAL PRINCIPLES

1. In accordance with the agreement on control machinery in Germany, supreme authority in Germany is exercised on instructions from their respective Governments, by the Commander in Chief of the Armed Forces of the United States of America, the United Kingdom, the Union of Soviet Socialist Republics, and the French Republic, each in his own zone of occupation, and also jointly, in matters affecting Germany as a whole, in their capacity as members of the Control Council.

2. So far as is practicable, there shall be uniformity of treatment of the German population throughout Germany.

3. The purposes of the occupation of Germany by which the Control Council shall be guided are:

(I) The complete disarmament and demilitarization of Germany and the elimination or control of all German industry that could be used for military production. To these ends:

(A) All German land, naval and air forces, the S.S., S.A., S.D., and Gestapo, with all their organizations, staffs and institutions, including the general staff, the officers' corps, reserve corps, military schools, war veterans' organizations and all other military and quasi-military organizations, together with all clubs and associations which serve to keep alive the military tradition in Germany, shall be completely and finally abolished in such manner as permanently to prevent the revival or reorganization of German militarism and nazism.

(B) All arms, ammunition and implements of war and all specialized facilities for their production shall be held at the disposal of the Allies or destroyed. The maintenance and production of all aircraft and all arms, ammunition and implements of war shall be prevented.

(II) To convince the German people that they have suffered a total military defeat and that they cannot escape responsibility for what they have brought upon themselves, since their own ruthless warfare and the fanatical Nazi resistance have destroyed German economy and made chaos and suffering inevitable.

(III) To destroy the National Socialist Party and its

affiliated and supervised organizations, to dissolve all Nazi institutions, to insure that they are not revived in any form, and to prevent all Nazi and militarist activity or propaganda.

(IV) To prepare for the eventual reconstruction of German political life on a democratic basis and for eventual peaceful cooperation in international life by Germany.

4. All Nazi laws which provided the basis of the Hitler regime or established discrimination on grounds of race, creed, or political opinion shall be abolished. No such discriminations, whether legal, administrative or otherwise, shall be tolerated.

5. War criminals and those who have participated in planning or carrying out Nazi enterprises involving or resulting in atrocities or war crimes shall be arrested and brought to judgment. Nazi leaders, influential Nazi supporters and high officials of Nazi organizations and institutions and any other persons dangerous to the occupation or its objectives shall be arrested and interned.

6. All members of the Nazi party who have been more than nominal participants in its activities and all other persons hostile to Allied purposes shall be removed from public and semi-public office and from positions of responsibility in important private undertakings. Such persons shall be replaced by persons who, by their political and moral qualities, are deemed capable of assisting in developing genuine democratic institutions in Germany.

7. German education shall be so controlled as completely to eliminate Nazi and militarist doctrines and to make possible the successful development of democratic ideas.

8. The judicial system will be reorganized in accordance with the principles of democracy, of justice under law, and of equal rights for all citizens without distinction of race, nationality or religion.

9. The administration of affairs in Germany should be directed toward the decentralization of the political structure and the development of local responsibility. To this end:

(I) Local self-government shall be restored throughout Germany on democratic principles and in particular through elective councils as rapidly as is consistent with military security and the purposes of military occupation;

(II) All democratic political parties with rights of assembly and of public discussions shall be allowed and encouraged throughout Germany;

(III) Representatives and elective principles shall be introduced into regional, provincial and state (land) administration as rapidly as may be justified by the successful application of these principles in local self-government;

(IV) For the time being no central German Government shall be established. Notwithstanding this, however, certain essential central German administrative departments, headed by state secretaries, shall be established, particularly in the fields of finance, transport, communications, foreign trade and industry. Such departments will act under the direction of the Control Council.

10. Subject to the necessity for maintaining military security, freedom of speech, press and religion shall be permitted, and religious institutions shall be respected. Subject likewise to the maintenance of military security, the formation of free trade unions shall be permitted.

B. ECONOMIC PRINCIPLES

11. In order to eliminate Germany's war potential, the production of arms, ammunition and implements of war as well as all types of aircraft and sea-going ships shall be prohibited and prevented. Production of metals, chemicals, machinery and other items that are directly necessary to a war economy shall be rigidly controlled and restricted to Germany's approved post-war peacetime needs to meet the objectives stated in Paragraph 15. Productive capacity not needed for permitted production shall be removed in accordance with the reparations plan recommended by the Allied Commission on reparations and approved by the Governments concerned, or if not removed shall be destroyed.

12. At the earliest practicable date the German economy shall be decentralized for the purpose of eliminating the present excessive concentration of economic power as exemplified in particular by cartels, syndicates, trusts and other monopolistic arrangements.

13. In organizing the German economy, primary emphasis

shall be given to the development of agriculture and peaceful domestic industries.

14. During the period of occupation Germany shall be treated as a single economic unit. To this end common policies shall be established in regard to:

(A) Mining and industrial production and allocations;
(B) Agriculture, forestry and fishing;
(C) Wages, prices and rationing;
(D) Import and export program for Germany as a whole;
(E) Currency and banking, central taxation and customs;
(F) Reparation and removal of industrial war potential;
(G) Transportation and communications.

In applying these policies account shall be taken, where appropriate, of varying local conditions.

15. Allied controls shall be imposed upon the German economy, but only to the extent necessary;

(A) To carry out programs of industrial disarmament and demilitarization, of reparations, and of approved exports and imports.

(B) To assure the production and maintenance of goods and services required to meet the needs of the occupying forces and displaced persons in Germany, and essential to maintain in Germany average living standards not exceeding the average of the standards of living of European counties. (European countries means all European countries, excluding the United Kingdom and the Union of Soviet Socialist Republics.)

(C) To insure in the manner determined by the Control Council the equitable distribution of essential commodities between the several zones so as to produce a balanced economy throughout Germany and reduce the need for imports.

(D) To control German industry and all economic and financial international transactions, including exports and imports, with the aim of preventing Germany from developing a war potential and of achieving the other objectives named herein.

(E) To control all German public or private scientific bodies, research and experimental institutions, laboratories, etc., connected with economic activities.

16. In the imposition and maintenance of economic con-

trols established by the Control Council German administrative machinery shall be created and the German authorities shall be required to the fullest extent practicable to proclaim and assume administration of such controls. Thus it should be brought home to the German people that the responsibility for the administration of such controls and any breakdown in these controls will rest with themselves. Any German controls which may run counter to the objectives of occupation will be prohibited.

17. Measures shall be promptly taken:

(A) To effect essential repair of transport;

(B) To enlarge coal production;

(C) To maximize agriculture output; and

(D) To effect emergency repair of housing and essential utilities.

18. Appropriate steps shall be taken by the Control Council to exercise control and the power of disposition over German-owned external assets not already under the control of United Nations which have taken part in the war against Germany.

19. Payment of reparations should leave enough resources to enable the German people to subsist without external assistance. In working out the economic balance of Germany the necessary means must be provided to pay for imports approved by the Control Council in Germany. The proceeds of exports from current production and stocks shall be available in the first place for payment for such imports.

The above clause will not apply to the equipment and products referred to in Paragraphs 4 (A) and 4 (B) of the reparations agreement.

IV. Reparations From Germany

In accordance with the Crimea decision that Germany be compelled to compensate to the greatest possible extent for the loss and suffering that she has caused to the United Nations and for which the German people cannot escape responsibility, the following agreement on reparations was reached:

1. Reparation claims of the U.S.S.R. shall be met by re-

movals from the zone of Germany occupied by the U.S.S.R. and from appropriate German external assets.

2. The U.S.S.R. undertakes to settle the reparation claims of Poland from its own share of reparations.

3. The reparation claims of the United States, the United Kingdom and other countries entitled to reparations shall be met from the western zones and from appropriate German external assets.

4. In addition to the reparations to be taken by the U.S.S.R. from its own zone of occupation, the U.S.S.R. shall receive additionally from the western zones:

(A) Fifteen per cent of such usable and complete industrial capital equipment, in the first place from the metallurgical, chemical and machine manufacturing industries, as is unnecessary for the German peace economy and should be removed from the western zones of Germany, in exchange for an equivalent value of food, coal, potash, zinc, timber, clay products, petroleum products and such other commodities as may be agreed upon.

(B) Ten per cent of such industrial capital equipment as is unnecessary for the German peace economy and should be removed from the western zones, to be transferred to the Soviet Government on reparations account without payment or exchange of any kind in return.

Removals of equipment as provided in (A) and (B) above shall be made simultaneously.

5. The amount of equipment to be removed from the western zones on account of reparations must be determined within six months from now at the latest.

6. Removals of industrial capital equipment shall begin as soon as possible and shall be completed within two years from the determination specified in Paragraph 5. The delivery of products covered by 4 (A) above shall begin as soon as possible and shall be made by the U.S.S.R. in agreed installments within five years of the date hereof. The determination of the amount and character of the industrial capital equipment unnecessary for the German peace economy and therefore available for reparations shall be made by the Control Council under policies fixed by the Allied Commission on Reparations, with the participation of France, subject to

the final approval of the zone commander in the zone from which the equipment is to be removed.

7. Prior to the fixing of the total amount of equipment subject to removal, advance deliveries shall be made in respect of such equipment as will be determined to be eligible for delivery in accordance with the procedure set forth in the last sentence of Paragraph 6.

8. The Soviet Government renounces all claims in respect of reparations to shares of German enterprises which are located in the western zones of occupation in Germany, as well as to German foreign assets in all countries, except those specified in Paragraph 9 below.

9. The Governments of the United Kingdom and the United States of America renounce their claims in respect of reparations to shares of German enterprises which are located in the eastern zone of occupation in Germany, as well as to German foreign assets in Bulgaria, Finland, Hungary, Rumania and eastern Austria.

10. The Soviet Government makes no claims to gold captured by the Allied troops in Germany.

V. Disposal of the German Navy and Merchant Marine

The Conference agreed in principle upon arrangements for the use and disposal of the surrendered German Fleet and merchant ships. It was decided that the three Governments would appoint experts to work out together detailed plans to give effect to the agreed principles. A further joint statement will be published simultaneously by the three Governments in due course.

VI. City of Koenigsberg and the Adjacent Area

The Conference examined a proposal by the Soviet Government that pending the final determination of territorial questions at the peace settlement the section of the western frontier of the Union of Soviet Socialist Republics which is adjacent to the Baltic Sea should pass from a point on the eastern shore of the Bay of Danzig to the east, north of

Braunsberg and Goldap, to the meeting point of the frontiers of Lithuania, the Polish Republic and East Prussia.

The Conference has agreed in principle to the proposal of the Soviet Government concerning the ultimate transfer to the Soviet Union of the city of Koenigsberg and the area adjacent to it as described above, subject to expert examination of the actual frontier.

The President of the United States and the British Prime Minister have declared that they will support the proposal of the Conference at the forthcoming peace settlement.

VII. War Criminals

The three Governments have taken note of the discussions which have been proceeding in recent weeks in London between British, United States, Soviet and French representatives with a view to reaching agreement on the methods of trial of those major war criminals whose crimes under the Moscow Declaration of October, 1943, have no particular geographical localization.

The three Governments reaffirm their intention to bring those criminals to swift and sure justice. They hope that the negotiations in London will result in speedy agreement being reached for this purpose, and they regard it as a matter of great importance that the trial of those major criminals should begin at the earliest possible date. The first list of defendants will be published before Sept. 1.

VIII. Austria

The Conference examined a proposal by the Soviet Government on the extension of the authority of the Austrian Provisional Government to all of Austria.

The three Governments agreed that they were prepared to examine this question after the entry of the British and American forces into the city of Vienna.

IX. Poland

The Conference considered questions relating to the Polish Provisional Government and the western boundary of Poland.

On the Polish Provisional Government of National Unity they defined their attitude in the following statement:

A—We have taken note with pleasure of the agreement reached among representative Poles from Poland and abroad which has made possible the formation, in accordance with the decisions reached at the Crimea Conference, of a Polish Provisional Government of National Unity recognized by the three Powers. The establishment by the British and United States Governments of diplomatic relations with the Polish Provisional Government has resulted in the withdrawal of their recognition from the former Polish Government in London, which no longer exists.

The British and United States Governments have taken measures to protect the interest of the Polish Provisional Government, as the recognized Government of the Polish State, in the property belonging to the Polish State located in their territories and under their control, whatever the form of this property may be. They have further taken measures to prevent alienation to third parties of such property. All proper facilities will be given to the Polish Provisional Government for the exercise of the ordinary legal remedies for the recovery of any property belonging to the Polish State which may have been wrongfully alienated.

The three Powers are anxious to assist the Polish Provisional Government in facilitating the return to Poland as soon as practicable of all Poles abroad who wish to go, including members of the Polish armed forces and the merchant marine. They expect that those Poles who return home shall be accorded personal and property rights on the same basis as all Polish citizens.

The three Powers note that the Polish Provisional Government, in accordance with the decisions of the Crimea Conference, has agreed to the holding of free and unfettered elections as soon as possible on the basis of universal suffrage and secret ballot in which all democratic and anti-Nazi parties shall have the right to take part and to put forward candidates and that representatives of the Allied press shall enjoy full freedom to report to the world upon developments in Poland before and during the elections.

B—The following agreement was reached on the western frontier of Poland:

In conformity with the agreement on Poland reached at the Crimea Conference the three heads of Government have sought the opinion of the Polish Provisional Government of National Unity in regard to the accession of territory in the north and west which Poland should receive. The president of the National Council of Poland and members of the Polish Provisional Government of National Unity have been received at the Conference and have fully presented their views. The three heads of Government reaffirm their opinion that the final delimitation of the western frontier of Poland should await the peace settlement.

The three heads of Government agree that, pending the final determination of Poland's western frontier, the former German territories east of a line running from the Baltic Sea immediately west of Swinemuende, and thence along the Oder River to the confluence of the western Neisse River and along the western Neisse to the Czechoslovak frontier, including that portion of East Prussia not placed under the administration of the Union of Soviet Socialist Republics in accordance with the understanding reached at this Conference and including the area of the former free city of Danzig, shall be under the administration of the Polish State and for such purposes should not be considered as part of the Soviet zone of occupation in Germany.

X. Conclusion of Peace Treaties and Admission to the United Nations Organization

The Conference agreed upon the following statement of common policy for establishing, as soon as possible, the conditions of lasting peace after victory in Europe:

The three Governments consider it desirable that the present anomalous position of Italy, Bulgaria, Finland, Hungary and Rumania should be terminated by the conclusion of peace treaties. They trust that the other interested Allied Governments will share these views.

For their part, the three Governments have included the preparation of a peace treaty for Italy as the first among the immediate important tasks to be undertaken by the new Council of Foreign Ministers. Italy was the first of the Axis powers to break with Germany, to whose defeat she has made a material contribution, and has now joined with the Allies in the struggle against Japan.

Italy has freed herself from the Fascist regime and is making good progress toward the re-establishment of a democratic government and institutions. The conclusion of such a peace treaty with a recognized and democratic Italian Government will make it possible for the three Governments to fulfill their desire to support an application from Italy for membership of the United Nations.

The three Governments have also charged the Council of Foreign Ministers with the task of preparing peace treaties for Bulgaria, Finland, Hungary and Rumania.

The conclusion of peace treaties with recognized democratic governments in these States will also enable the three Governments to support applications from them for membership of the United Nations. The three Governments agree to examine, each separately in the near future, in the light of the conditions then prevailing, the establishment of diplomatic relations with Finland, Rumania, Bulgaria and Hungary to the extent possible prior to the conclusion of peace treaties with those countries.

The three Governments have no doubt that in view of the changed conditions resulting from the termination of the war in Europe, representatives of the Allied press will enjoy full freedom to report to the world upon developments in Rumania, Bulgaria, Hungary and Finland.

As regards the admission of other States into the United Nations organization, Article 4 of the Charter of the United Nations declared that:

"1. Membership in the United Nations is open to all other peace-loving States who accept the obligations contained in the present Charter and, in the judgment of the organization, are able and willing to carry out these obligations;

"2. The admission of any such State to membership in the United Nations will be effected by a decision of the General Assembly upon the recommendation of the Security Council."

The three Governments, so far as they are concerned, will support applications for membership from those States which have remained neutral during the war and which fulfill the qualifications set out above.

The three Governments feel bound, however, to make it clear that they for their part would not favor any application for membership put forward by the present Spanish Government, which, having been founded with the support of the Axis Powers, does not, in view of its origins, its nature, its record and its close association with the aggressor States, possess the qualifications necessary to justify such membership.

XI. Territorial Trusteeships

The Conference examined a proposal by the Soviet Government concerning trusteeship territories as defined in the decision of the Crimea Conference and in the Charter of the United Nations Organization.

After an exchange of views on this question it was decided that the disposition of any former Italian territories was one to be decided in connection with the preparation of a peace treaty for Italy and that the question of Italian territory would be considered by the September council of Ministers of Foreign Affairs.

XII. Revised Allied Control Commission Procedure in Rumania, Bulgaria, and Hungary

The three Governments took note that the Soviet representatives on the Allied Control Commissions in Rumania, Bulgaria and Hungary have communicated to their United Kingdom and United States colleagues proposals for improving the work of the control commission, now that hostilities in Europe have ceased.

The three Governments agreed that the revision of the procedures of the Allied Control Commissions in these countries would now be undertaken, taking into account the interests and responsibilities of the three Governments which together presented the terms of armistice to the respective countries, and accepting as a basis the agreed proposals.

XIII. Orderly Transfers of German Populations

The Conference reached the following agreement on the removal of Germans from Poland, Czechoslovakia and Hungary:

The three Governments, having considered the question in all its aspects, recognize that the transfer to Germany of German populations, or elements thereof, remaining in Poland, Czechoslovakia and Hungary, will have to be undertaken. They agree that any transfers that take place should be effected in an orderly and humane manner.

Since the influx of a large number of Germans into Germany would increase the burden already resting on the occupying authorities, they consider that the Allied Control Council in Germany should in the first instance examine the problem with special regard to the question of the equitable distribution of these Germans among the several zones of occupation. They are accordingly instructing their respective representatives on the control council to report to their Governments as soon as possible the extent to which such persons have already entered Germany from Poland, Czechoslovakia and Hungary, and to submit an estimate of the time and rate at which further transfers could be carried out, having regard to the present situation in Germany.

The Czechoslovak Government, the Polish Provisional Government and the control council in Hungary are at the same time being informed of the above and are being requested meanwhile to suspend further expulsions pending the examination by the Governments concerned of the report from their representatives on the control council.

XIV. Military Talks

During the conference there were meetings between the Chiefs of Staff of the three Governments on military matters of common interest.

Approved:

J. V. Stalin,
Harry S. Truman,
C. R. Attlee.

Index

Set in Linotype Electra
Format by A. W. Rushmore
Manufactured by The Haddon Craftsmen
Published by HARPER & BROTHERS
New York and London